WOUNDED HeaLeR:
memoirs & poems of a BROKeN BOY

Terrance {Cirvant} French

Table Of Contents

Foreword

Acknowledgments

FOREWORD

Although this is supposed to be a Foreword for my friend Terrance {Cirvant} French, I wish it were an Afterward. For how could I possibly introduce Terrance and his story any better than he does in the pages that follow? What I can say is that this book will undoubtedly move you. The way Terrance presents his story is not intended for shock value or to be sensational. In fact, that is what is so moving about it; the ordinariness of the raw dysfunction in Terrance's story unmasks the reality of similar dysfunctions in all our experiences...regardless of how "raw" yours and my life has been to date. The themes of life have a universal tenor and I suspect you, like me, will find yourself in the pages that follow. You might even encounter God. I did.

The power of theology in biography is on full display here. Terrance stands tall as the wounded healer, the powerful preacher, the proclaiming prophet, and the salt of the earth all rolled into a singular journey with God in this life. And if you listen closely you will hear the ancient Scriptures, the promises of God with us, finding voice in the poems and scenes contained herein. This book is an outflow of the promise contained in James 5:16 – *Confess your sins one to another that you may be healed.* Terrance has mastered the blunt act of confession. This book gives testament to that fact. But as a friend, I can assert that I have witnessed the ongoing healing that simple act has afforded in his life. It is so potent in fact I have even become willing to try it myself. Thank you, Terrance, for confessing. In so doing, I hear God...and that moves me to action. May all hearers and readers be so moved!

Jared Black

I always wanted to write a book about my life. Initially I thought I would write a book chronicling my life as a struggling "Man of God" who overcame "The Evil" and now is pursuing "The Good" . I envisioned Oprah would call me to interview me about my controversial way of looking at my life and the things I have endured. The church would rally behind me and be excited about my stance against all we believe is evil. I would be celebrated because I learned to tell the difference and I choose the good.

Well, this is not that book. This is my story in Memoirs and Poems, as honest as I can be.

Acknowledgments

This Book is Dedicated to my Mom (Deborah French) and Mama (Gail Francis Page).

I would like to thank the many people who have journeyed with me as I've written this book. I started writing 12 years ago as a freshman in University. This has been an amazing journey of writing and re-writing. I have learned much about myself in the process. Writing has served to heal things in me I did not know were broken. My prayer is that it does the same for readers.

Tamara Fyke, you are my sister, friend and crazy amazing editor. Thanks for being a part of my journey. You help make this possible. Jared Black, I am so honored to call you friend and brother. Thanks for being consistent and honest in my life. You have been a tremendous help in calling me into who I am. Dave Fitzpatrick, thanks for taking so much time to listen and guide me. Your voice in my life has been an answer to prayer. Thank you also to the many who sow into my trips, Those who believed in me when I did not believe in myself. Roshun Eppenger thanks for being led. Ryan "Cape Town Brown" Dalton, thanks for helping me get the bones of this project out of my head. Diogo Siebert and Tyler Hartshorn thanks for sharing your artistic giftings. My family, thank you for your love and support. I wrote this for the One in Six men who carry wounds of brokenness. Healing is possible.

Thirsty

I Thirst
I thirst like our sisters who thirst for that which they know not of
And they pour out all their worth for unrealistic love
Cause he says, "Baby I love you and shoot you know how we do..."
So she opens up her legs for every man that wishes to deposit seed
And with every child they conceive comes shame guilt and hurt
And he's out the door cause he don't love her like that no more
And now she's all alone to raise his kids with no life to call her
own and she's thirsty
I'm Thirsty...

I thirst like a junkie feenin' for crack, cause I'm trying to escape
where I am at...
And with each hit I can forget about what he did...
Cause you don't know what its like when your step dad comes in
late at night...
And he's supposed to tuck you in but he wants to make you a real
man
See that's why I slept with her and her and him and them
Cause there has been something missing inside of me since then
And I'm trying to get it back
I'm thirsty... I thirst

I thirst like a kid that acts out in school
And I think its cool when they call me a fool
Cause at least they're paying attention to me
See where I come from you gotta keep it real
And I can't tell my mom how I feel
Cause she got too much to worry about
I mean my little sisters staying out too late at night
My brothers going to jail for trying to sell moms is catching
And my dad he could help out is what my mom say
But his wife is mad about the child support they have to pay
So he only comes down to whoop my butt for acting like a class

clown
When all I want is for him to be around and I'm thirsty
I Thirst...

I thirst like a 12 year old in a miniskirt
And I'm hoping that my too little clothes will hide the hurt
Because nobody validates me at home
So I'm hoping that validation will come thru Jerome or Tyrone
Or somebody will tell me I look good
Make me feel good like every little girl should
Cause my mom ain't got time for me
See her and her boyfriend just broke up last week
She's trying to get with the neighbors man from down the street
She heard he be getting paid and he just got a new Escalade
And Mr. Wadale from down the street said that I should come to his house and sleep
Especially when my mom ain't home cause a pretty little thing like me don't need to be alone
I know they call him Chester but he don't look like no molester and I'm thirsty

"Ho, yea who thirst come to the waters..."
"Ye which have no money come buy and eat..."
Won't have to sell myself
No longer will I seek men wealth
I can know love for real
"Why spend money on that which is not bread
And work and labor for that which does not satisfy"
See we are all like the women at the well...We're thirsty
And like her we try and feel out thirst with something natural
So she goes through husbands 1, 2, 3, 4, 5...
And now she is living a lie cause there is a void inside of us that only God can fill

See I lost my mother when I was 12 years old
I felt like I was slipping into a black hole
And my dad wasn't around to try and console

I was that kid that was just plain bad
But it was a facade me being angry and mad
I was hurting and I was in pain
And nobody gave me a hug or tried to ease my pain
You are just another no good Nigger is what they all thought
Just another victim of the ghetto so give the white man all the fault
So I tried to fill my void with sex and drinking and all that I was
worth I was searching
I heard the call "Come ye who Thirst!" and I forsook all
Cause if their was anyway I could be free I would risk it all to task
one ounce of victory
And I... I see Jesus on the cross and I hear him cry out... I thirst
I realize that his thirst is not for something natural but for God's
will to be fulfilled
Cause he knew that we would be thirsty too
So when He cries out "It is finished" He quenches our thirst anew

Come ye who thirst and receive Love, He quenches
Come ye who thirst and receive grace, He quenches
Why spend money on that which is not bread
And work and labor for that which does not satisfy
Our thirst was quenched when Jesus died
Why thirst when he is living Water.
No longer thirsty.

Chapter 1
Loss

She Everything

My Mama is Everything
I need for nothing
She hugs me when I need it
I know her love
Spank me when I need
Making sure I grow up right
Send me to church
Want me to know Jesus
She cook my favorite meal
Beef Stew and Hot Water Cornbread
She everything
Send me to school
So I'm gon' be smart
Told me to make a white friend
Tell me, "Be better than I am"
She work and cook
Buy me things
May not be the newest shoes
She buy what she can
Listen to me sing
Tell me "Sing the 'Golden Girl' theme song"
Smile bright looking at me
She proud
Know she making me something
Told me I can be somebody
My Mama, She Everything

I remember the day my mother died like it was yesterday... August 17,1993. The sun shone brightly that morning, though the day was gloomy. It was a few days before school was supposed to start. I was twelve years old and full of mixed emotions. I had the initial excitement of going into the seventh grade and the dread of the end of summer. I was starting a new year of football that day. Though I was anticipating practice, I had the weirdest feeling. It felt like the whole world was moving, and I was stuck in one moment.

My mother had been sick for the last few months. I watched her go from a nicely shaped woman with curly hair, who obviously considered her appearance, into her present look. She had lost nearly a hundred pounds and looked ill. Her hair, which she loved, was gone leaving a thin patch on the top of her head. Her face was sunken in due to her massive weight lost. Her skin clung to her bones; it was as if I saw every bone. She managed to comb her thin patch of hair back. The sore on her upper lip looked as if it were healing. She lay on the couch too weak and too feeble to move. My sisters, my cousins, and I played video games loudly at the foot of the couch. My mother sat silently.

Since my mother was not able to take care of my sisters and I, our entire family had been staying with my aunt and great-grandmother. My mother had become so sick she struggled to look after herself. As we played video games, the phone rang. She made no effort to answer it. I raced into the kitchen to answer the phone. It was my mother's nurse. She sounded very friendly and obviously Southern. The nurse called to remind my mother that she was to visit shortly.

Soon after the phone call the nurse arrived, a short white lady with long blonde hair. She wore blue jeans and a Nike t-shirt. I remember it well because not many white people visited us then. We all looked surprised that she was not in uniform. We stared intently as she took my mother's temperature. As we watched her, I noticed her facial expression change. Her pleasant smile turned into a look of disbelief and subdued shock. Calmly, she picked up the phone and dialed the numbers. I could not hear what she said, but it sounded important. She moved around nervously asking my mother questions.

An ambulance arrived not long after the nurse made the call. The sirens from the vehicle rang fear into my heart. I still remember the way my mother looked as the men from the ambulance lifted her onto the stretcher. Her eyes stared weakly at me. Those eyes that once looked at me with love now held fear. I remember looking into her eyes and seeing her soul. It was as if I could literally see her pain. The pain and hurt I saw was not for her. It was for my sisters and me. I saw the tears swell in her eyes as she looked at me. I felt her pain and shared her hurt. Though she whispered not a word as they wheeled her out, I heard everything she said. While I watched her leave the words she rehearsed in my ear that past year played in my heart. "If anything ever happens to me, take care of your sisters," she would say. It was at that moment that I realized this would be the last moment we would share. My life as I knew it was about to change forever.

I went to football practice that day but never left that moment entirely. The rest of the day I thought of an encounter I had the prior year. I woke up one night to a man dressed in white standing over me. He was dressed similar to a General in the military with many flags on his chest. He was white with brown hair combed back into place. His face was stern yet gentle, chiseled. He stood at ease with his arms behind his back. He looked to be strong but compassionate, and I was not afraid of him at all. I was almost at peace by the presence of this "man" as he stood over me. As I looked up at him, he conveyed to me my mother was going to die. His lips did not move but I felt words, like impressions, inside me. As he looked at me I knew what he was saying without one verbal word being uttered. I knew he was sent to deliver a message. At that point I was not aware of my mother's sickness. That night I remember begging the Lord quietly to give her more time. As discreetly as the man came, he left.

The memory of that encounter haunted me my entire football practice. I went through practice like I was waiting for something to happen. I was distracted by the knowing, the expecting. I knew the exact moment my mother died. I felt it. My body was going through the motions of football drills. I was running to catch the ball on a catching drill. The coach threw the ball, and as I grabbed it and pulled it to my chest something struck in me. Time stood still, I was stuck in midair. I knew that moment as I grasped the ball that she was gone.

I whispered to myself, "My momma just died."

I did not say a word to my friends or teammates. It felt like life and reality had been sucked out of the world. The world I knew was gone. It was like I was dreaming.

All that had ever seemed right now felt like a movie. I was a character, not a person. I was playing a role but yearning to know the truth behind the character. I knew she was gone but how was I to live without her? I was quiet the remainder of practice. The entire ride home from football practice I thought of my mother. I was like a zombie on that ride, stuck in a dream. How does one live in this new world? When I reached my drop off spot I was met by some of my neighborhood friends. When they saw me on the truck they yelled my name, trying to get my attention. I did not respond. I knew what they wanted to tell me. I did not want to hear it. I wanted to not be anymore. Instead, I wanted to be away from this new world.

When I finally got off the back of the truck they tried to tell me. Before they could complete their sentences I answered, "I know."

"How you know?" they responded.

I did not answer. They followed me home. I walked fast, nearly leaving them behind, not shedding a tear. They followed me, astounded at our interaction. I needed to get back to reality. I needed home to be the way it was. I rushed to my great-grandmother's home, hoping it would wake me.

When I arrived at the front yard of the house there were people everywhere. They spilled over from the house to the yard. People I had not seen in years were chatting and laughing. I made my way to the house, not acknowledging any of them. Silencing them with my presence, I was on a mission. I needed to hear something that would shake the dream I was in. I needed someone to wake me up from the nightmare. My sisters were on the couch crying, and I joined them…still not shedding one tear. My body was quaking. The room was full of noise, yet I don't remember a sound. I sat there, right foot propped on the side of the table, shaking and trying to wake up.

I kept thinking, "This has to be a dream. How can I know a life without her? How can I exist while she is gone?" Waiting for the dream to end, I could not cry. It had to be a dream, I thought.

The night was filled with attempts to lift my spirits. It seemed everyone had a story of an exciting time in his or her life that was shared with my mother. Some people gave words of comfort, but the phrase repeated most throughout the night was ever so memorable, "Don't cry. You have to be strong for your sisters." I do not think that people were aware of the gravity of this statement. How does one make this request of someone so young? It felt to me like they were asking me not to feel. I was okay with it. It had to be a dream. My uncles on both my mother and father's side made their attempts to give stories of how it was for them to lose their parents. Although they meant well, it was not something I cared to relive with them.

My dad made it to town from Indiana, and, as always, I was glad to see him. Seeing him was like breathing for the first time. He was my hero and I knew he could wake me from this nightmare. It was almost as if I was not aware that I was still alive. I thought he could make it all go away. I was hoping that he would save me from this dream.

My sisters and I spent that first night with my dad at his sister's place. Although it was late, we spent a couple of hours playing. I hid under the covers playing with my dad and sisters. It was in that moment when I was alone under the covers that reality hit. I was alone and my mother was no more. This was not a dream. I felt the blankets covering my face…the movements of my sisters beside me…the smell of my aunt's place was too familiar. I was not dreaming. She left me. My mother was gone.

My dad tried to pull the blanket from my head playfully, and I struggled with him. When he removed the blanket covering me, my face was full of tears. He took me outside promptly to avoid my sisters seeing me cry. We sat on my aunt's back porch and he tried to comfort me. He repeated what was told to me throughout the night, "You have to be strong for your sisters." I did not sleep much at all that night. I could not handle the pain.

The day after my mother passed was harder. The walk from the car to Granny Lizbeth's, my great-grandmother's, house was tough. As I walked through the front yard of the brownstone, all eyes were on me. I walked, trying not to feel people's pity. My eyes looked straight ahead, trying not to make eye contact. As I walked, pain grabbed me again. I aimed to make it to the apartment without shedding a tear or speaking a word. I made it to the house without conversation. When I reached my cousin's room, I cried myself to sleep.

Later that day I had one of the hardest conversations with my Granny Lizbeth. She has been in the hospital with her own medical conditions at the time of my mother's death. When she called home my aunt answered the phone and told me to pick it up. I took the phone call upstairs to have some privacy. As soon as I said hello and heard her call my name, we both immediately burst into tears. She called me "Big Ole Man." When she spoke, it was like we felt one anothers pain. I could hear the hurt in her voice, and I felt the pain in her heart. It was the same pain I felt. She finally managed to speak through her tears.

"You got to be strong for your sisters" she said.

After we got off the phone, I managed to wipe my tears and pull myself together before returning to join my family…trying my best to hide the pain.

I spent most of my time alone lying in the bedroom crying that day. It was time away from my sisters and the obligation to be strong. I was trying to grieve my mother back to us. My aunt Mary came over to try to get me to eat. At first I could not. I felt physically incapable. After a few attempts, I finally came around.

She made me a ham sandwich and told me, "I know it hurts, but you gotta eat something."

Death was pain and loss that could not be changed or eased. I wanted my mother, and I had no idea how to get her back. I ate the sandwich staring into space…trying to breathe and feel anything other than hurt.

The day of the funeral is a vague memory, like those before her death. I only remember glimpses. I recall the female attendant from the funeral home. She wore so much makeup she looked like she jumped out of a casket herself. The church looked different then it did on Sunday mornings. The room felt different. There were no happy songs, no joy or laughter, only tears and sadness. Granny Lizbeth took it hardest. During the funeral she repeatedly cried out to the casket, "I'll be there soon." While we sat there in the middle of funeral, I remember looking at the casket and being angry at my mother. I did not cry, the hurt was gone now, just anger.

As I stared at the women in the casket all I could think was that is not my mother. Being so full of anger, I could not contain it any longer. "That's not my momma," I said loud enough for my aunt Cherry on the pew in front of me to hear.
She turned to look at me, "That's her," she whispered.

My mother was wearing a wig due to her hair loss. My oldest cousin took me by my arm and led me to the restroom to comfort me.

"Man, that's her, it's her," he said as he slid down the wall in tears.

It was then I saw that he was hurting. He had also lost someone too. I looked at him in pain and could not cry…wondering how this could happen to us.

When we went back into the sanctuary the funeral was ending. I took a seat next to my paternal grandmother in the back of the sanctuary. The pallbearers began to roll the casket away. As they wheeled her out I realized this was reality, she was gone. For the first time that night I cried. My dad's mom held me to her chest. It was then, at that moment I lost my mother, and I lost my childhood. When they wheeled her casket away I realized there was no grieving her back. She could not get up and ease my pain. They were taking her and my hope of waking up from this dream with her.

The night after the burial we sat on Granny Lizbeth's front porch. The crowds were gone; now it was just family. My sisters and I had been asked the day my mother died where we would like to live. We were given two choices. We could either move to Indiana with our dad or stay in Nashville with our aunts Mary and Cherry. We chose to stay in Nashville. Choosing to stay in a place familiar and that we had always known to be home came easy. Indiana had always bored us. However, we were just children. My sisters were ten and seven, and I was twelve. As children we are not always able to choose what is best for ourselves.

My dad had come over to tell us that he was leaving and heading back to Indiana. He and I walked down the sidewalk towards the van he was to ride in. As we walked, he asked me if I was sure I didn't want to come with him. In my heart, I was wishing that he would stay, and I would not have to make the decision. I told him that I wanted to stay. I hoped that he would say he would stay with us.

After I told him, he began to instruct me, "Take care of your sisters. I wish I could stay, but I have to go to work."

When I close my eyes, I can still see him getting in the van and closing the doors behind him. I can still feel him pulling off. I felt like I was stranded on an island and the only person who could help me was sailing away.

I never needed my dad when my mom was alive. We always knew he was around, but my mom had been everything to us. In that moment as he pulled off, I felt for the first time like he had abandoned me. I had to fend for myself. The only way that I could rationalize what was happening was by telling myself that he had chosen his new family in Indiana over me. As he pulled off he reminded me one more time to take care of my sisters. For the first time, my hero let me down.

The day after my dad left we moved into Granny Lizbeth's house. It was hard for me to go into my mother's house, so I did not help much. While moving my uncles were throwing away things we no longer needed. I remember them bringing my mother's royal blue carpet towards the house and showing it to my aunt. It was the carpet that once covered my mother's floor in our old apartment. It had been rolled up, unused in the newer apartment. They unrolled it to show my aunt and were surprised by what they found. Inside it were newborn baby mice. My aunt told them to throw the carpet away. I was overcome with emotion at the thought of them throwing anything of hers away.

I angrily yelled at my aunt, "That's my Mama's!"

She tried to explain to me that we could not keep everything. I could not watch as they moved the remainder of things. I was somehow attached to it all. As they threw away things I felt like they were throwing my mother away. I was losing her with each item. I let her go that night. She had to not exist for me to function around my family. There was no more remembering her. Granny Lizbeth had become delusional with her sickness. Once while my cousin Keisha and I sat watching over her she asked for Shirley, her daughter and our grandmother. My maternal grandmother Shirley died when my mother was twelve. We were afraid so we ran across the yard to our elder cousin Betty's home so she could console Granny Lizbeth. We knew that if people start talking to or asking for people who were dead, death was coming. She had suffered many years from one sickness or another. Betty came over to sit with her.

Granny Lizbeth had spent many years in pain. Late at night she would cry to the Lord, "Lord, have mercy. Help me! Help me!" Her pleas to God would rend any heart. Then she would call to one of us to come and help her. She had back spasms and would be in so much pain it was nearly unbearable. One of us would come and rub her back where the pain was until she could manage to fall asleep. I still remember the sound of her voice calling.

A few months after we moved into Granny Lizbeth's, she died. Hearing she died was like a ton of bricks hitting and crushing me. There were mixed emotions in me. I was glad that her suffering was over, but to me it was like losing my mother again. I cried more at her funeral than I did at my mother's. I thought about her reaction at my mother's funeral. She now had joined my mother as she told her she would.

When my mother and great-grandmother died in the same year the joy of the holidays went with them. We set a place at the table for them both at Thanksgiving dinner. The house was thick with grief. It was quiet. We all grieved with no tears…only sighs. We all were hurting, but no one spoke of the pain. They were gone, and we had to face it. How do you breathe when the air has been sucked out of you? That day was suffocating. That became my life…what living felt like. I struggled to breathe and to keep living even though life seemed like it was over. I was angry that year. I was angry at my mother, God and anyone I could find.

Every Christmas my mother's side of the family would get together on Christmas Eve. It had always been my favorite holiday. My aunt Mary would bake cinnamon rolls, pies and cookies. We would drink hot chocolate and eggnog. Sometimes we would sing and dance. That night each of the kids could open one gift before bed. It was just our family. That night was our family time. It was full of life and joy before that year. The year of their deaths was different. That joy left me when they died.

My Strength

She called me hers and I was
Stubborn with love
Strong as Man
She carried me
She was my strength

Can you be loved and not know it?
Touched and not remember?
Wind ripping through city
Water past dam
Love washing over me
She was my strength

Face bringing peace
Hugs calming me
Voice easing my pain
Embrace like the rain
Causing nurture
She was my strength

Like sun at night
Peace in war
Comfort in pain
Not present
She is no longer
But she was my strength

Chapter Two
Pictures Not Film

Home

Brick Floor
Walls same
Nail-holes
Reminder of those before
Cold on my feet
Hard this place
Stale this air
Steps of concrete
Welcome mat at feet
Blaring box fan
Helps my Sleep
Propped in window
Tied with metal hanger
Leaning over my bed
Keeping me cool in heat
This was Home

I don't remember a lot before the death of my mother. I think I blocked it out. Those times before her death are like flashes to me, pictures instead of film, glances instead of vivid depictions of time well-spent.

What I do remember of my mother was her strength. She was the youngest of her siblings. She gave birth to me when she was sixteen and died when she was twenty-eight. In those twelve years she loved me. In those years, she was my everything.

When I was born, we all lived in one Housing Project apartment. The apartment was five bedrooms, housing my great grandmother, my mother's three brothers, my aunt Cherry, her four children, and my aunt Mary and her daughter. I have a vague memory of this and only know it as truth through stories.

What I do remember about it was breakfast. Often breakfast was some sort of cereal. We used powdered milk or a can of condensed milk mixed with water. We had to be careful pouring the cereal… along with the cereal came small water bugs, little black ones that we picked out before pouring the milk. We learned to pick out as many as we could, but often there were too many to pick through. The milk and extra sugar masked any taste of the remainders.
Another morning ritual in the house was coffee. I have been drinking coffee for as long as I can remember. I would get my own cup and saucer and drink with my great-grandmother. I have continued this ritual throughout my life. My paternal grandmother was also a coffee lover and would allow me the pleasure.

We moved into our own project apartment when I was still very young. It was before my mom had my youngest sister. The apartment had two bedrooms. I still remember the day we moved in.
My cousin Tweet and I played outside. As we played, we met some of my new neighbors, whom I had seen throughout the neighborhood. We peed from the front porch to the yard, and one of the girls came over saying, "What are ya'll doing?" Funny, we were only around

four or five, but mischievous. We lived in that house for many years.

The older people in our neighborhood called our apartments "The White Projects". They called the apartments across the street from us "The Colored Projects." I was told that many years before I was born white people lived in our apartments. There are a few differences in the two sets of project apartments. The White Projects have bigger rooms and bathrooms…more space. The Colored Projects are smaller, and some rooms can only fit a twin bed with barely enough room to walk by.

I remember our apartment being very clean…a drastic contrast to a lot of our neighbors. The walls were cinder blocks painted white and near glossy, a thick white paint that dripped like glue. The floors were an ugly tile that my mom covered with carpet. The apartments were rigid and hard when empty, almost industrial…brick and concrete painted white.

My mother made those walls, brick and concrete, home. It was our safe place. The apartment was the only place I ever lived with my father. He lived with us a short while before he left. My dad moved away when I was quite young. I don't have many memories of him ever living with us…couple of flashes, but nothing I can hold on to. I remember being picked on by neighbors and him forcing me back outside to face them…telling me to fight back or get my butt whooped by him. This was hood life.

After my father moved away, my sisters and I were sent to Indiana each summer to spend time with him. Though we hated Indiana, we loved taking the trip to see our father. For us our father was like any other father, a superhero. When he came to Nashville to visit, it was like Christmas had come all over again…partially because we were so excited to see him, and partially because he actually came like he said he would. As a child I always expected him not to come through, an expectation that didn't often disappoint.

Although I have heaps of memories with my dad's family, I don't hold many with him. There are only a few memories of spending time in Indiana, a theme park or watching movies at his house. I have a couple of him coming back to see us. One of getting in trouble as a kid on one of his visits home, and him taking Big Paul's, my grandfather's, belt and whooping me. I don't remember what it was for, but that is what I remember.

I knew my mother to be everything I now know a father was to be. She was a provider, protector, nurturer. My fondest memories of her I see in flashes…watching her dress and do her hair, Michael Jackson blaring in the background, "I'm talking to the man in the mirror." She was my light. Snapshots of her standing in the mirror pinning her Jerry-curl into place…the walks from our home to my great grandmother's apartment that we would take nearly every day. My mom walked with her signature washcloth draped over her shoulder as my sisters and I played ahead of her. There was one day I let a kitten into the house and my sisters and my mom stood atop of the couch screaming for me to get it out, and I looked from the doorway, stunned at their reaction to the kitten. Memories in pictures, not film.

When my mom became sick she started to come to church. Before then she would only send my sisters and me with our cousins. During those times my prayer during Sunday School would be, "Jesus, please get Todd out of our house," which often provoked laughter from my cousins, but it was a sincere prayer. Todd was my mother's boyfriend. From the day I met him something in me didn't approve of him.

My mother would often ask me questions like, "Why don't you like him? Why do you treat him like he's not here?"

I didn't have an answer. My sisters connected easily with him, but for me he was a plague that had invaded our family. I wanted to get rid of him.

26

When my mother became ill she joined us on Sunday mornings, often to my surprise. I was elated in the beginning. I had been singing in the choir for a while then and my mom had only come once to hear me sing a solo. Now she was here every Sunday. She was present, yet disappearing before our eyes as she lost weight. Finally, the day I hoped for came. She walked down the aisle to give her life to Jesus and to be baptized. I remember she wore a black top and a brown wrap-skirt. Her stockings were loose, ill-fitting due to her weight loss. I remember it like my mind had taken a picture of that moment. Her standing with her head bowed at the altar.

The day she was baptized was the happiest I had ever seen her. Our church did not house a baptismal pool so we used our mother church's, First Baptist Church of Downtown Nashville. This was the same church in which my cousins, friends and I had been baptized a couple of years earlier. Now from those pews I sat and watched my mother being baptized in that very same pool. When she came up from the water, she lifted her hands and screamed with excitement, smile as big as the day and joy just as infectious. I feigned embarrassment at her excitement, but inside I was overjoyed. My mother became a different woman after that. I remember her in flashes…like pictures streaming.

Because she was sick, some nights we would stay with my great-grandmother and aunt. They remained in the apartment I once called home. Late one night while lying down in the living room to sleep, my mom called me on her way to the restroom. She told me to get up and walk with her up the steps.

As we walked, she whispered, "You have to stay away from them, and not be like them. They are evil," referring to my uncles.

It must have been a result of the medicines, but she seemed to be a different person that night. I knew she loved them…she was trying to protect me.

When we got to the bathroom, I sat on the tub as she used the restroom, almost dazed by this woman in front of me. She asked me what Psalm Twenty-three said. I tried to recite it; she rehearsed it with me. I said it afraid, not of her but of the moment.

When we finished she repeated, as she had so often during this time, "You have to take care of your sisters, if anything happens to me"… words a mother, a dying mother, leaves her son to guide him.

From that day on she grew smaller and smaller…so small that she would park at the back of my great-grandmother's apartment so she didn't have to walk in the front yard where people could see her. She was so thin that she looked like a walking skeleton. During those times, HIV/AIDS patients were treated with chemotherapy medicines, which some say, essentially created one of the saddest genocides in America.

When my mother became so weak she couldn't walk, she had to use a wheelchair. When she was not in the hospital she continued to come to church. On Sundays my older cousin, Baby Brother, would carry her into the sanctuary. She was a ghost of the woman she had been months earlier, daunting braids weaved into the thin patch of hair she had left.

The summer before my mother died she sent me to stay with my dad. What was normally a two-week summer trip had become her way of preparing me for a life without her. Without our knowledge she had intended for me to stay with my dad throughout the summer and to not return home to Tennessee until after she died. Her plan would eventually become known. I hated it in Indianapolis as a kid. It was boring place for me and somewhat lonely. I often missed all my friends in Tennessee. I complained a lot, and my boredom was apparent. Frustrated, my dad sent me back to Tennessee, without my mother's permission or knowledge. I rode to Tennessee with my dad's older cousins, and they dropped me off in Celina.
Celina was my dad's hometown. A small country town a couple of

hours drive from Nashville. I was used to spending summer weeks there. There was miscommunication as to how I would get back to Nashville, so I spent a couple of weeks in Celina before I made it home back to the big city. When I got there I walked into my great-grandmother's house. My mom lay in my great-grandmother's bed. I walked into the room where she was. She was the thinnest I'd ever seen her. She turned to see me in the doorway. Instead of being welcomed with delight, I was greeted with frustrated anger.

"What are you doing here?" she said angrily. "How did you get here?" She burst into tears.

I left the doorway. Confused, I sat in the living room and cried.

My aunt Mary walked through the door and asked, "Boy, what's wrong with you?"

Through my tears I told her what had happened with my mom. My aunt went back to talk with my mother and I heard the conversation. "Why'd you say that to that boy?" my aunt asked.

My mother told her plain. She had sent me away because she needed my dad to teach me how to be a man. She wanted him to take care of me. It was then I realized that I wasn't supposed to have come back.

They talked and then my mother called me back to the room. She hugged me and apologized…an embrace I still can feel…bones embracing me. She was near quivering from weakness…pulling me…the smell of her medicine overtaking me….the fear of her sores going through my mind….my mind choosing to not be in the moment. It's only in moments of recollections like this that I can see how much she loved me.

The day I found out about my mother's sickness I remember like flash photos….a flash you shield your eyes from. I slept-over at my great-grandmothers house the night before while my sisters and mom stayed home. My cousins were outside playing. I sat in the living room and watched TV. I had become more of an introvert since my mother had become sick. My mother and sisters moved to a new apartment in our complex while I was away at camp that summer, but this had already become home for me. I hated to see my mom in the condition she was in and I think I was also embarrassed. While watching TV I heard whispering in the kitchen. Whispering was not common in this house. I overheard them say my mother's name.

I slowly made my way to the kitchen to find my aunt and cousin Keisha having a conversation at the sink while washing dishes. They stood side by side talking. In a very quiet tone my aunt conveyed to Keisha what HIV was, piquing my interest even more. At that time I heard very little of this disease. Something in me knew to whom they were referring to, but I needed to hear them say it.

My cousin asked, "So that's what Deborah has. Did she get it from Todd?"

I felt faint, like all the air had been sucked out of the room. Something in me knew my mother was not getting better. She lied, just like I thought.
My mother had before alluded to having cancer, but she said she would get better. This was after telling me she might be pregnant with step-father's child. I saw her disappearing before me and knew she didn't have long. She tried to assure me she would be fine. Standing there hearing them talk angered me. I left the kitchen doorway quietly and slipped out of the house not knowing if they knew I had been listening.

I made my way to my mother's house, not speaking to neighbors, not acknowledging friends. I was on a mission. I needed to know the truth from her. I needed my mother to tell me the truth. I found my mother in her bed. The house quiet and dark like it was waiting for me. I think the mix of anger and frustration had overtaken me.

30

The reality of whom I had come to confront finally hit me.

My mother demanded respect from my sisters and me. We knew better than to disrespect her. My mother would knock me out if I told her she lied to me. When I entered the house I made my way to my room to think. The house was quiet…only the sound of my mother's TV playing in the other room. I sat in the room alone… the house felt empty. I looked through the many unpacked boxes in what was to be my room. I had not slept there since they moved in.

While looking around I saw boxes that didn't look like my things. The boxes seemed to be calling me…drawing me in, so I looked through them. I think something in me was searching for answers. Scavenging through one box that was not mine I found what I was looking for. I found a pamphlet that read "How to Protect Yourself". Seeing it was like being hit in my chest. In the pamphlet I saw pictures of how to use condoms…graphic images of a penis with a condom on it. Inside it I saw the word AIDS, and my heart broke. I felt like I had been punched in the chest. Why would my mother have this?

The anger that carried me to the house seized me. I stepped into my mother's doorway and waited for her to look at me. My shoulder resting on the doorway… my head tilted to the side. Her room was dark…she lay in bed watching TV. Her eyes made their way to me.

"You lied," I said to her. I spoke words in a tone I normally would not dare speak to my mother. Her gaze became a look of shock. "You lied," I repeated, full of emotion.

"What are you talking about, boy?" She managed to get up. She was too weak to walk now…barely enough energy to lift herself up.

I held up the pamphlets not wanting to let her know I had overheard my aunt and cousin talking.

"This says AIDS! You told me you were going to get better. You lied," I said as I stormed to the next room not waiting for her response.

I heard her call me, "Terry! Terry!" She called, and I did not answer. She was too weak to come after me…I was too hurt to care.

I lay in what was to be my room…tears slowly making their way down my face. These are the memories I hold of my mother before her death. I can't see them stream in my mind. I see them in pictorial glimpses…pictures…not film strips.

Sugar Bread

You take two pieces of bread
Bunny Wrapped
Lite or White
Brown is for white folks
Opening twisted tight
No Bugs
Put up from mice
Check to see no green
Pull off any
"Little mold never hurt nobody"
Granny yells
Pull off the edges
Get the sugar in that jar
Make sure there ain't no coffee droppings
Take your bread and pour sugar on one slice
Now rub'um together
Make sure you over the sugar jar
Now eat that
Lunch
Sugar Bread

Chapter Three
Like Music

Dear Son

Dear Son,
I will no longer be with you. Well when you read this I'll be gone.
So, I pray that while I'm gone you can be strong. Make me proud.
Act right, mind your mama and take care of your sisters. You are
the man of the house now, so hold it down.

In my absence I leave you... Well, all that I have to give. The
feeling of not having a father around to care. The pain of thinking
you aren't good enough for me to stay. The responsibility of being a
man before your time, I leave you...

The obligation of being a father figure to your sisters. All my
issues I pass on to you. I'm sorry I cannot be around son. I have
to do what's best for me. I will see you when I can, if it's only to
reprimand you or whoop your butt. We can talk via phone, just to
make sure you minding you mama.

I know you will struggle with who you are because I won't be
around to tell you. Don't be nobody's punk! Ain't no punk in me.
I'm your daddy, I don't care what other nigga come in the house,
don't forget that.

Son, I won't be around to protect you, just don't let it hurt you too
bad. Hey, I know you are young but don't let no tears fall, man up!
Get all the girls you can get. Just make sure you strap up, be a man
do your thang!

I can't protect your innocence, man, no one protected mine. So
be strong. Be a better man than I am. As you get older I probably
will call less, still, don't call me by my first name show me some
respect, I'm your daddy! I may not be at any of your games or
school plays. Just make sure you represent. Make your daddy
proud!

Love, Your Dad

Before my mom's death, we spent most of our time with my mom's side of the family, so, naturally, after she died my sisters and I had chosen to stay with her sisters. I chose to stay with the eldest of the sisters in the same house as my great-grandmother. This had already become home to me before Momma died. My mother had a tight-knit family. Her siblings were composed of two sisters and three brothers.

My maternal grandmother was murdered by my grandfather's girlfriend. My mother's father died a year before my mother died. All I knew of him was that he was an alcoholic. He would stay with us occasionally. The smell of liquor was pungent, coming through his pores. His signature drink was "Wild Irish Rose"…the name I only knew from seeing his half-pint sized bottle whenever he was around. As I kid I knew my mother's sisters were hard-working women. Her brothers were either drug users, alcoholics or a combination of the two. The entire family lived in the same housing project neighborhood.

The same housing project community had been home for most of my family their entire lives. I did not know it as Government Housing… it was just home. My aunts and uncles all lived just a building away from each other. When I was young, it was a safe place for me. Though everyone rented apartments, people talked like they owned them. This place served as home for most families generation after generation.

Our project home was a five-bedroom apartment. We shared it with my aunt, her four children, and two of my uncles. We all lived dispersed throughout the house. One of my uncles lived in the hallway closet. For the first few months after my mom and my great-grandmother died, my cousins, sisters and I all slept with my aunt in her room, mostly because of fear of the dead.

We heard stories of people coming back to visit their family after their death. A good friend of mine lost his mother a couple of years before me, and he would tell me stories of what he thought was his mother coming into his room to check his homework. We also heard stories of things that would move in the night signaling a visitation from beyond. I wasn't sure if it was imagination or reality, but either way, as much as I wanted my mother back I did not want her coming in the middle of the night.

My aunt Cherry was the quietest and most reserved of her siblings. Though she was the oldest she stayed more in the background. As a child my memories of her are mostly her going to work, coming home, and drinking beer until she fell asleep. We would always joke that we could smell the beer coming through her pores. I don't think she was prepared for the challenge of having three more kids when she took us in. My great-grandmother had always been around to help her with her children. Now she was on her own.

One night not long after my mom died I lay in my bed, which by this time was across from my aunt's room. I couldn't sleep that night. I lay in my bed crying, trying my best not to be heard…silent pain. Tears…I try and catch before they hit the pillow. *Brave One*…in tears. I was weeping and yearning for my mother. I felt hopeless. The grief I felt seemed to grasp me.

I crawled down from the top bunk and made my way across the hall to my aunt's room. It was a quiet night. The house was dark… everyone was asleep. I didn't hear the normal loud outside noises that night. As I walked, I could only hear my footsteps. When I entered my aunt's room I stood over her bedside whispering her name, trying not to break down in the silence. I whispered her name again and again. Finally, she woke up.

"I miss my Momma… I want my Momma," I managed to get out and wait for the pain to abate…it didn't. The words leaving like a prayer…tears stream like water, flowing. My heart raced…my chest felt like it was about to cave in.

I stood crying, sighing my pain. My aunt looked at me and from her bed she whispered, "I know. Me too."

I stood there for a moment, feeling alone, hoping that God will say, "Ok, I'm sorry…here she is." I wished she would come in and hold me or that I would wake up from the nightmare that had again taken me…wake up to see her at home cooking for me and my sisters. When nothing happened I made my way quietly back to my room. I crawled to the top bunk and cried myself to sleep.

It was settled…I would never share my pain again. I developed a very short temper after that. I was angry at the world. It didn't take much for me to fight anyone. In school I became known as a troublemaker. At home, though I lived with my family, I grew distant. I began to resent my sisters. I would watch them fight, and I would try not to care. I hated that I could not make them behave like my mom could. My mother had always told me to take care of them, and I thought I was failing. I was angry that my dad left me with the responsibility.

My aunt's house was pretty rambunctious. There wasn't a week that went by that some sort of drama didn't occur. Something was always brewing, whether it was arguing between one of the kids and our uncles. Often it was me threatening to pack all my clothes and run away…or the backlash of me being suspended from school time and time again. There was never a dull moment.

My uncles that lived with us were both addicts. Drug addiction was just a part of life for us. Eventually my youngest sister went to live with my mother's other sister, Mary. My middle sister and I stayed with Cherry. It became hard for me because we had only known life together as siblings, yet as time passed they became like a memory. I pulled away because they reminded me of all I felt I needed to forget. They reminded me of what was the past.

When I saw my sisters I could see my mother's face. When I saw them I was reminded that I was supposed to take care of them. I wanted to erase all that was before…the pain of knowing that I was alone in this world without a mother. So without knowing what I was doing, I built walls against them in my life to shelter myself and to ward off the pain. I wanted to forget that I ever had a mom who loved me. I hated that I saw her in them. I hated that I felt responsible for them. These walls served to shield me…these walls made them disappear.

We all took on different lives after our mom died. Each of us became vastly different, a far cry from the children my mother had reared. The discipline she had instilled was now a fleeting memory. I was the troublemaker in school, whose comfort was in music and books. My middle sister, who looks the most like my mother and took on most of her personality and stubbornness, became a fighter, often in some after school brawl. My youngest sister was seven when my mom died. As she grew older she spiraled into trouble. She cycled through group homes to juvenile detention centers. Prior to my mother's death we had always been good kids. Now we had become known as troublesome.

For my mother's side of the family the death of two of the strongest women had become too much. I think for all of us, or at least me, we were waiting for them to return. For me to cope, my life had to become a routine.

There were days where I could barely maintain my pain after school. I remember one day coming home feeling like I was going to explode. I made my way to my room. Some of my family members sat in the living room. My uncle glared at me through the corner of his eyes while making sure his eyes were still on the TV screen. I climbed my way to the top of the steps hoping not to be noticed, but yearning to be acknowledged. Feeling like I was not really there. I had become a ghost. I wondered if they would notice if I chose not to come home. I reached my room and entered my safe house.

With the close of my room door behind me came safety…solace…I could breathe. It felt like I had been waiting to breathe all day. And with that breath came tears that I could not draw back. I sank to the floor, trying to cover my mouth so my deep belly cry would not be heard…I was hurting. Realizing that the sound of my pain was too great, I crawled to my stereo and blared Boys II Men. "I miss her…I want my Momma" I cried to the air softly with feeling, hoping that just maybe God will hear.

My mother came home that day out of the blue. It surprised me. Yet, even while surprised, it was like it was like I was expecting it. I hugged her tight that day, and she smiled.

"You remembered I told you to take care of your sisters, didn't you?" she said.

I never forgot, I thought, and we went home. My sisters did not come home with us that day…it was our time. We went to our old apartment, the one we lived in when she was healthy. The place was still furnished. That night took the cake. She made me Beef Stew… she knew it was my favorite. I don't remember much more about that night other than that she was there. My Momma came back home to be with me. I woke up the next morning to my aunt's yells from downstairs. My mother was gone again. It had been a dream. I had fallen asleep. My room was my place of escape and safety.

Music became my comfort, whether it was blaring Boys II Men or NII Deep "I Miss You" to mask my cries in my room or singing in the church choir. Music was my way of escape. I had joined the church choir when I was nine. I remember the day I tried out to be in the choir. My friends convinced me to face my fears and join. I was incredibly shy growing up. Deede, my older cousin, was the church Choir President. She was a mean relative that we feared as kids. Everyone in the neighborhood knew not to sit on her porch or she would come out and put you off. Our family kept our church afloat.

I knew in order to get in the choir I had to go through her, so with much peer pressure I went.

That afternoon we all sat around her front porch in chairs, and I sang the song we had rehearsed nearly the whole day. My friends and I had been singing at middle school track across the street from our neighborhood. We sang "Fill my cup, let it overflow". I recited the ad-libs I had so often heard her sing in church. After we finished there was a pause, waiting for her response. This was one of the first real interactions I had ever had with her...the others were her sending me to the corner store with a note for a Pepsi and a pack of cigarettes. I did not know how she would react. Normally you have to be twelve to join the choir, but she made a exception for me because I could "hold a note" and would make a good tenor.

"We'll give you a try, but you betta act right!" she said.

I joined the choir and church became my life. No longer did I have to be sent to church. It was a place I longed to be.

Monday night choir rehearsals became a ritual that me and my cousins still talk about to this day. It was the night Fresh Prince came on and we would try and make our way back home in time to catch the show. I was the youngest in the choir and often on Sundays the only male. Sister Stevenson and I would hold the tenor section down. She had been the only tenor before me.

It never failed that whatever church we would visit as a choir we would get compliments. The small group of us were no more than twelve on a good day. People would say, "You guys sounded like a big ole choir!" It was in the company of these people that my love for music flourished. I would listen to how each of them led songs and learn.

When I wasn't singing in the choir, my friends and I continued with our mission of starting our own boy band. We would rehearse often after school and every weekend. We would start with the secular songs, and finally give up and just go back to gospel. We rehearsed consistently for months without reason. Finally we had our first opportunity to sing somewhere. We had an invitation to sing at Mark's church, Greater Mount Zion. After our first performance the pastor decided to take us under his wing and help us out a little bit.

Pastor Finch was a good friend of Bobby Jones, and a great singer in his own right. When we weren't meeting with him, we still rehearsed on our own. For some reason they always made me sing bass, initially. And then one day after seeing a stage play, Mark's mom had this idea that we could sing one of the songs she'd heard an older gentleman sing in a play. The song was "I Know I've Been Changed", and I was to take the lead.

So in the kitchen of Mark's grandmother's apartment, I took my first stab at leading the group. We began to sing more often in those days, in evening services or youth events. We would always use "I Know I've Been Changed" to get the crowd riled up. These guys became my brothers. We did not know a life without each other. We did not know a life without music. Before my mom died, she beamed when she heard of me singing in the choir. Those days I remember she would always try to get me to sing, and I would tell her come to church to hear me. Those were happy days when I was a kid just like my friends…no different.

Music would also play a major part in changing my life….March 20th, 1994 the day of my church's annual Calendar Tea. I say that like I know what it means, to me it was another evening service we put on to host other choirs. Sundays like those were my favorite. It seems something wild always happened in the evening services that we just did not get in the mornings. Someone was always bound to "catch the Holy Ghost" or "get happy."

I remember the first time I sat next to someone that got happy. It was at a choir concert. I watched as she sang and moved down the aisle stunned at feeling something else was in the room I could not see. I was familiar with seeing it happen occasionally at Church and as kids we would always laugh. It was always something to see…people making a spectacle of themselves…yelling…sometimes dancing and running down the aisles for reasons I did not understand. We had no idea what was happening other than being told, she just got happy. I was always scared of getting happy, but I liked to watch other people from a distance. As a kid I wanted to watch from a distance because if it got to close I thought it would jump on me.

It seems in that time the only thing that seemed to give me some peace, aside from my room, was the church. Suspension from school was a normal occurrence…becoming more normal with each week. That day, March 20th, I was singing lead on a song the choir had been rehearsing for quite some time. The air was full of excitement to have so many people in our small building.

Those were my quiet days…I spoke very little. My conversations were more with my friends or in my room with God asking Him, to please give me my mother back. Since she had been gone no one mentioned her to me. I used to wonder if they forgot her. It's like she never existed. I remembered her by the pain and grief I felt. I would hear whispers that stopped when I came into the room. She was gone…I was in pain…and no one noticed.

Music had become my hiding place. With a blank face and no enthusiasm, I was going to lead a song. I wondered if people could see that I had listened to the song over a hundred times to learn the words. The title of it was "Jesus Stepped In" by the William Brothers. I was nervous to sing in front of so many people, but my mother's family had come out to see me sing. My sisters were in the back of the church with my aunt Cherry, who only came to these events.

As I sang the song I remember feeling my heart racing. I lost myself in the song. It became much more than words…it was prayer that seized me. I connected with the words, and they became my plea to God. I needed Him to step in. I poured myself out in that song. As I sang I felt the atmosphere change, and then something happened in and through me. I was acting completely out of character. What happened next was a spiritual event that would shake me.

As I sang I noticed I could see myself and the choir outside me. It was like I left my body and I watched as I sang. It felt like I was watching someone else on the stage singing. Throughout the room people yelled and clapped but I heard not a word of it. I could not even hear the sounds I was making or the song I sang. There was complete silence. I saw myself singing on stage with passion and emotion I had not seen before. Then suddenly I was back in my body. It was like I was trying to find a way to see through my eyes again.

There were still no sounds…just a peace that I felt. My eyes looked open to me, yet others tell me later they were closed. I saw my feet moving…dancing down the aisle…I had left the stage. My braids were bouncing in my face. I saw the people in the congregation clap and scream and cry and dance by…but no sound…just peace and quiet.

I danced to the hallway and closed my eyes, waking up on the floor. My older cousin Betty stood over me.
"He needed that," she said.
Someone lifted me up and put me in a chair. I sat in the chair in shock at what had happened. Stunned by the way I felt. It was like light and peace had washed over me. I felt different. I sat there for a few moments alone knowing Who had done this to me. I never wanted that feeling to leave. I had "caught the Holy Ghost" or "got to shouting" people told me. All I knew was something happened so real in me. In that moment, the pain was gone. I had peace and excitement. That day shook everything in me.

Peace

I prayed with my body
Hands lifted like pain
Offering. Sacrifice
Wet my face
Vexing my soul
Sound released through me
No words
Groaning my desire
My arms become my prayer
Wrapping them around myself
Hoping. Yearning
My feet echoing
My prayer. No words
Stomping my fervor
Let me be heard
My heart and tears
My prayer
Let Heaven come
I become my prayer
And He spoke quietly
Within the noise
Answering me like blanket
Wrapping around me
Peace

Chapter Four
Where I'm From

Games We Play

"Ice in A Cup," yelled
"Kool-Aid," Response
Humid day
Like kids
We play
Face pressed against tree
Bark gripping my face
Eyes Covered
"Ready or Not, Here I Come!"
And we run
Like nothing else exist but the chase
Games we play

Like
"Down by the riverside, Silver rock saying Michael Jackson don't
wear no socks"
Hand slapping
Laughter and time escapes us
From hands to thumb
"Pow Wow Ding Dong"
Struggling to get the best
"So step back White Girl you don't shine, I gotta Colored girl to
kick you behind"

Games we play
Unaware of meanings
Colored means with crayons, right?
"Pamela Pamela Pamela little Biscuit"
Smiling
"Shame Shame Shame, I don't wanna go to Messico"
I think we meant Mexico
"No more more more"

Two players Only
Switched
"Big fat Filet-o-Fish, Quarter Pounder, French Fries"
Competition Made
"Concen..."
Clap Clap Clap
"..tration"
Intent on the win
Humid Day
Just Kids
Just Play

In our neighborhood we were afforded different opportunities. The youth center that I often played at after school had a tutoring program. Each Thursday night, members of the affiliated Church of Christ would come down and tutor kids from my neighborhood. My friends and I often would go…some for tutoring and others for the attention we would get from the white people who came to tutor us.

For me tutoring was a chore, until I met one particular lady on a Thursday night. Her name was Miss Diana. She became my go-to tutor every Thursday night. It was in these sessions that we connected. I remember one Thursday night she didn't show up… it had an impact on me emotionally. I covered my face and cried. I didn't want to be tutored by anyone else. I longed for the attention I got on Thursday.

The next week when she came back she invited me to her house over the weekend. I was excited about the opportunity. The weekend finally came. Miss Diana and her husband came to fetch me from my apartment to take me to their house. She was an older white woman with two sons and a daughter.

I remember pulling up to their house and thinking it was a mansion. For me, suburban life was a dream world. At their house we had a picnic on the back patio. Miss Diana introduced me to their pet rabbit named Barbeque. We spent the day playing in the backyard in her kids' playhouse. It was during visits to Miss Diana's house that I gained the freedom to imagine and to dream…it was there I began to write.

Miss Diana and I would sit at her computer, side by side. She would tell me to tell her a story. I was not used to imagining things. I was only used to my reality, the reality of hood life. It took some prying initially, but finally I began reciting a story to her. It wasn't as profound as a Tolkien story. It must have been about a dog and a boy or some dream world. When I was done, she printed the story off with a title page that included these words "written by Terrance French". I became a storyteller.

Although my time with Miss Diana's family opened my eyes to a new world, my neighborhood was home. Playtime was often creative. We played the normal games: kickball, red light-green light and red rover. Often the guys would get together and play backyard football or a baseball game called fly-and-bounce. We became more and more creative in ways to have fun. In our housing projects, pets were not allowed, so often on Saturday mornings my friends and I would make our way into the single family houses closest to the projects to find puppies to play with. We would travel through alleyways and backyards, finding puppies we thought needed attention. It was often easy to find puppies birthed from stray dogs.

A few times we took the puppies from the owners' backyards…if the mother dog had more than one. We would bring them home only to have to return them after our parents found out, but for at least one day we had pet puppies…if only for that day. One weekend on our puppy escapades we came upon a family of three puppies. My cousins, nicknamed Tweet and Bunch, my friend Darnell and I got them from an alleyway. When I say 'got them' from the alleyway, I really mean one distracted the mother while the others took each puppy one-by-one from the back of someone's house. We were a mischievous group.

When we finally had the puppies home we put what little money we could find together and bought dog food for them. We were pet owners for the little time we had them. Bunch, my older cousin is mildly mentally challenged. He would often listen and do what we told him to, but when we made him angry he would react violently. This particular evening, I don't know what happened, but he grew angry with us over the puppies. He took one of the puppies from us and threw it up in the air as high as he could. He was abnormally strong when angry. We all watched, stunned at what was happening. When the puppy came down it made a squeaky sound and,

50

miraculously, was still alive. We decided after that incident that he was not allowed to go with us when we went to get pets. Not only because we feared he might kill them, but he also ate the dog food. We returned the puppies promptly after the event.

We played other games that were normal to most kids in any neighborhood, like hide-and-go-seek, only, it was of the sexual nature. We called it "Hide-And-Go-Get." I think because in our homes most of us had little to no protection of our innocence, we were exposed to a lot of adult subjects and content even as babies. I can remember being as young a seven and having some sort of sex with girls my age. Even in those encounters we would act out either what we had seen, or what some of us had had done to us by others. We called it "hunching" or "getting-booty"…names we heard as kids but really didn't know what it was.

I think I was more sheltered than a lot of the kids in our neighborhood. For me, dry humping was considered sex, but the more I hung with other kids the more I was exposed to what was their norm. As young as seven-years-old, we were having penetrated sex…sometimes in groups…or sneaking away in closets or in bushes for one-on-one sexual encounters. Mostly the girls led in the exploits. Some girls as young as ten were more experienced than some adults I know today. In a neighborhood where education is not promoted, and where our parents were teenagers themselves, we saw things we should have been protected from.

By the age of five or six, most of my friends had seen porn…guys and girls. A lot had sexual experiences with people who were much older than them…their friends or people in the house. Some had been touched in ways children should never be touched. This was our reality. I remember my first time seeing pornography. I must have been five or six-years-old. I wasn't able to read, but I remember my friends and I finding a book, and in the book it had pictures of naked women in various positions. We took the book and looked through it, hiding it from our parents yet captivated by the images that we saw. None of us had reached puberty…we didn't know how to process what our eyes had seen.

It was not until I reached middle school that I had my first sex education class in the fifth grade. By then it was too late. I had participated in more sexual encounters than I could have counted…a lot before puberty. This is the culture created when the innocence of children is not protected. This is the atmosphere created when kids become parents. It is what results when the eyes and the hearts of our children are not shielded, and they are handed things that they are not capable of carrying. I can still remember some of those situations very vividly, but in remembering I do not see any parents around to correct, to guide, or to teach.

When we weren't being mischievous we spent time playing with friends in the backyards of our apartments. In my preteen years I became more artistic. My group of friends was creative. We spent time either making up or rehearsing dance routines or creating songs. Mark was the older guy in the group, and he and I often led the way. Our group changed directions often. We went from step team to full on dance team within a week. After that we created singing groups with two different missions in life. One group sang secular music and we called that group Masterpiece, a name I got off a Lays Potato chip pack. The other group was a gospel group called God's Creation. The latter of the two was the one we actually took on…we began singing gospel around Nashville.

One day while dancing in the backyard we experienced something that would shake us. We had our radio plugged in at Mark's apartment, which was one brownstone over from the one I stayed in with my aunt. Each brownstones' back door faced each other. That day we danced as normal… forgetting the world around us…just dancing, creating as we always did. During one break from dancing we saw a fight happening across the street near the playground. The day seemed weird. The air seemed to disappear. It was like watching a movie, a horror film.

Seeing what was happening across the street, we rushed to the gate to watch the fight.

Mark hurried to put the radio inside the house as we all stood at the gate watching the fight. There were three older guys, two on the ground fighting and one standing over them yelling. I could not hear what he was yelling. I don't remember hearing any noise actually. It was silent, like time moved in slow motion. As they fought suddenly the one standing over took out a gun and shot the guy lying on the ground. It happened…quick…in an instant. I don't remember hearing the gunshot. I do not know how many shots were fired…if it was one or more. I cannot remember hearing any noise actually… just seeing it in silence and moving slowly.

We took off running. All of us ran to Mark's house initially. We had become accustomed to running at the sound of gunshots. We had actually turned it into sort of a game, like a race…racing for our lives and laughing when it was safe. The winner was the one who got to the porch or inside the house the fastest. There was never a thought that we could die from the gunshots or that it could bring harm. It was just a game…a game we played through out most of our childhood. Growing up as we grew up this was normal. We did not know a different way of living.

We all ran into Mark's house since it was the closest. After we felt it was okay I left Mark's house and walked through our back door through the house. I told my aunt what happened, and we both walked out our front door towards the scene. When I got there I saw heaps of people walking towards the play park. I never expected what we saw. Even after seeing the shot, I was not prepared. I joined the crowds of walking people…the emotion from onlookers was heavy in the air. I walked alongside my aunt towards the street. As we walked the man who pulled the trigger came walking behind us. He walked casually and nonchalantly…like he was just another guy. Seeing him made my heart stop, but we kept walking.

We joined the crowd of people who stood looking towards the body that lay in the grass. The cops had already arrived. As we walked towards where the body laid the mother of the guy lying on the ground was brought to the scene. She was held up by two women… one on either side of her. She was crying hysterically. Her grief was tangible. Tears erupted from nearly everyone watching. I realized who the young man was. He was just a few years older than me…a kid. As we stood watching the adults, frustrated that his body still lay out, all I could think was, "I hate this place." For the first time in my life, the place that I had always known as home felt like a prison to me.

The body lay in the field finally covered by the officers. They were waiting for the coroners. Standing and looking almost unable to move, I noticed a black officer in plain clothes with his badge around his neck walking in the crowd. He was asking whether anyone witnessed the shooting. I stood with my aunt and with my friends. Next to us were a couple of white officers. And as we stood there, I heard one officer whisper to the other, "One less nigger." From then on, I knew I had to escape this place. The game was no longer a game.

My Reality

I am 12 yrs old and my mother is gone...God rest her soul
My Dad?!, that dude ain't been around for as long as I can
remember
And now It's just me and my little sisters, And I feel alone
I know everybody's telling me to be strong and that I am a man
now
But I feel like a boy on the inside..
Be strong, you gotta be strong for your sisters they say
And so I set my face
Wipe my tears, and tuck away the pain until I can no longer feel
And now here I am, I am 12 years old and I cannot for the life of
me understand why this grown man is slipping his hands into my
pants
Ssshhh, he whispers and I know it's wrong yet I lay quiet and still
Cause at least he is paying attention to me
And he is taking my innocence
And I, I know that after this I will cry
And I hope that just maybe I will feel again
Be strong, be strong they say
and now my outer shell is hard as rock, You're a man now
Yet on the inside I feel like I am just a boy
And I miss my mothers touch
Cause since she's been gone there have been no hugs
No one touches me
I am no ones little boy
I am a man, who feels like a little boy on the inside
How does that feel?... he whispers...
And I lay quiet and still and I think
Maybe this is love, and then I miss my mothers touch
So I close my eyes too scared to move
And not strong enough to speak
I am 12 yrs old and in this moment I feel like something inside of
me is about to die...
This is my Reality

Chapter Five
Country Life

Her Hands

Her hands like strength and weakness
All made one
Holding my face
Cradling my youth
All that is her age holding me
She has gathered wisdom in these hands
Through years of use
Folding. Working. Mopping. Sweeping.
Lifting her young ones
Burns now healed
From meals past cooked
As she cradles my face
Using her thumb she wipes tears
These tears of mine she catches as they fall
These hands strong yet fragile
Hold Jesus in book
Soft and strong
The scent of Vaseline and butterscotch
Embracing me
Pinching my check
Swatting my butt
Thumb licked
Spit cleaning my smudge
Nail polish chipped nails
Warmth on my cheeks
Letting me know I'm safe
Hush baby, I'm here
Whispers, Granny's got you…
These hands…
Validating love in me
Making me know I'm here and wanted
I'm alive and belong to somebody
Hands, God made
Rearing me
Clapping to celebrate me…
These hands…
Those hands
Her hands

My dad's family was from a small town in Tennessee called Celina. We would often spend a great deal of family time there during the summers or holidays. We referred to the small country town only as "The Country". I remember spending some of the happiest moments in life there. It was a time for us to escape the hectic life and to embrace the country life.

My dad's side of the family was the opposite of my mom's side. Instead of being drug users my uncles and aunt were drug dealers. I was the oldest grandchild on my dad's side, so my grandmother spoiled me near rotten. My grandmother, Granny Gail, had six children. My father was the eldest of them. My uncles were more like older brothers than uncles to me. It was more like I was the baby of the bunch as opposed to the nephew, so much so that I called my grandmother, Mama. Granny Gail would always tell stories of when I was a baby. She boasted about how everyone would be so careful with me because they knew they would be in trouble with her if they were not.

Our family owned a little farm, where we raised chickens, pigs, and sometimes goats. One of the highlights of spending time there for us as kids was waking up early in the morning to feed the pigs or, as we called it, slopping the hogs. This small country place took on two different personas. For the young it was a place of safety and freedom… stark contrast to hood life. We had the freedom to travel and roam the hills. There was no big need for supervision…we were among family. Yet on the flip side the small town laid the backdrop for my family's drug operation. Celina, a town known for being the home of the oldest black church in American History, had become known as a drug haven.

My family had two trailer homes on top of a hill in the community called Free Hills. One home we called Granddaddy Big's trailer…it was a home that my great-grandparents lived in before he died. The second we called Granny Vera's trailer…it was the trailer that my great-grandmother lived in after the death of my great-grandfather.

Free Hills was home for most of my father's relatives. My cousins and I would spend many summer days walking the hills or riding our go-karts and four-wheelers up and down the roads. The place allowed a freedom we did not feel in our neighborhood. We were free to lose ourselves and just be kids.

We were always told fables of the woman who lived down the road from my Granny Vera's trailer. My older cousins would tell us she was a witch. Her name was Dorothy May. We were told countless stories of how she had disappeared in Celina and miraculously appeared at the courts of Cookeville thirty minutes away. There were tales of her turning policemen into frogs...things that seemed impossible yet made us fear her. These stories recounted by adults who seemed to believe just as ardently as we or at least pretended to. This woman for us was mysterious yet intriguing, generating many fear-induced nights of storytelling.

One fall day my younger cousin Mannie and I rode the go-kart around the roads. We were spending Thanksgiving with Granny Vera that year. We had just passed the Church-House, and we were approaching the hill to our great-grandmother's . In order to get to Granny Vera's trailer we had to pass Dorothy May's house. Suddenly from the woods appeared Dorothy May. She stepped out from the trees wrapped in blankets. I am sure she had a reasonable explanation as to why she was there but to us she just seemed to appear from nowhere. Without saying a word to one another my cousin and I knew we had to get away from this woman. A quiet fear overtook us. When we passed her we looked at each other and then back at her. I could see the fear in Mannie's eyes. In that moment our greatest fear happened, she looked back at us.

When Dorthy May looked the go-kart engine cut off immediately. I doubt this happened because she looked at us. It may have been just a figment of our imagination, but at that moment the engine went dead. When that happened we jumped off the go-kart and ran towards Granny Vera's trailer. We didn't look back to see if the go-kart was rolling back down the hill nor did we care. We just knew the witch was at work.

We made it to the trailer and were met by our cousins and uncle on the front porch.

My Uncle Ebo, in his very southern accent asked, "What's wrong wich yawl?" when we got to the stairs.

Struggling to catch our breath, we relayed to him that we had just encountered the witch. We told them our horror story and how she cut the go-kart off by looking at us. Uncle Ebo looked at us half-amused but more confused, and said chuckling, "Ya'll crazy!"

He went to retrieve the go-kart as we watched in dismay. We wondered if she would make him disappear. A few minutes later we sat laughing at what had just happened. To this day the story is that her glance killed our engine.

As a child Free Hills provided a life for me that most in my community were not used to. Often my cousins and I there would go on hiking trips around the property. Although there weren't many places to hike we would create adventures. It was a place full of possibilities, yet the night held noises we had never heard in the city. There was no fear of guns, no thoughts of drive-by's...it was my safe place... aside from the fear of Dorthy May.

The highlight of Celina is the annual homecoming. It's the church homecoming celebration that has expanded into a sort of family reunion for all of those connected to Free Hills. Each year we all gather back to the School-House, dance the night away at the "Disco" and spend Sunday morning at the Church-House. After church we have a big dinner. We end the weekend at Dale Hollow Lake... swimming the day away.

Spending so much time playing and having adventures, we were unaware of the drug deals going on right around us. My family kept it away from us. I knew as young as I could remember that my dad's family was dealing. In the neighborhood, it was well known who they were. My uncle would drive through the street and people would come out just to see the car he was driving. But, for me, there was no feeling of it being right or wrong. It was what it was…reality.

This Be Reality

This is the reality of ghettos, trailer-parks, townships and slums
world-wide
Even in the suburbs these are the cries… This is not a fable, not
just a story to entertain

Somebody scream genocide or murder
Something yell cry something!
Pain. Tears. Empty
Pain. Empty. Tears
I am empty.
Gone. Inside me its gone.
I couldn't do it on my own Scream for me…
I hurt but I can't keep it
Sick, I feel…Wash it away
It's not whole, they say
Just cells or tissue no soul they say
But why do I feel it deeper in me
Scream murder!

Pain. Empty.
These tears.
It was in me and I couldn't… Pain.
I had to get rid of it. Tears.
I got three babies that I struggle to take care of..Empty.
Its gone. I cant say he or her no… Scream for me.
This is Reality

Like Candy…the first taste
Entering me with pain at first then pleasure
Like a kind of blissful pleasure
Silent. Ecstasy. Overwhelming me.
I want more. Now I can't live without it.
In needles. Powder however I can get it
I'm lost without it

Unwanted and longing...It calls me
Do whatever you like to me, I need it.
Like Candy, the first taste
Now it eats me away...

This is the reality of ghettos, trailer-parks, townships and slums
world-wide
even in the suburbs these are the cries... This is not a fable, not
just a story to entertain
This is Reality

Chapter Six
Breaking Me

We Were Once Innocent

We once Loved
Once felt clean
We played like day had no end
Laughed like it mattered
Smiled with nothing hidden
And stood like no one was watching
We once were innocent

Once hugged and thought we shared love
Touched and knew we had encountered
And you once loved us without condition
Once cradled us in arm
Glowed just holding child near
Sang songs to connect to who we were
We once were loved

Once Sang like fear didn't exist
Spoke like our words mattered
Danced like leaves through air
We were present
Flesh. Bone.
But also heart and feelings
Soul and care
Emotion
Innocence

Music and Church were now my passions. I longed for opportunities to sing or to be in church to listen to other choirs and groups sing. I would spend countless Sunday evenings or weekends in choir concerts or church musicals. As a kid, my cousins and close friends all grew up in the church. We enjoyed the music and watching people get happy, shout and dance around the church. The events were never disappointing. I would often join in the dancing and shouting.

A choir my best-friend's aunt was a part of eventually extended their choir into a youth choir. It was their choir anniversary and they asked if I would like to join. I was elated. The first day we went to rehearsal was exciting. We were all asked to sing short parts of a song so we could be placed in vocal sections. When it was my turn I sang the song as I had been used to at my church. The director seemed surprised I could actually hold the tenor note. He placed me in the tenor section and gave me the male lead on one of the songs.

A lot of us kids became close to the choir director. We sang with them again for their Christmas concert. Next door to the director lived a few guys who also sang with us. We became friends with the guys. We spent many nights at the director's house hanging out and sleeping over. He was openly gay and had a boyfriend. We never felt threatened by him or his lifestyle. To most of us he was like an uncle. We were free to roam his house, play music, or watch movies. It was our escape from rules and our parents/guardians. One night while spending time there, things changed. The place I knew to be safe and kid-friendly became something different to me.

There was a jacuzzi in the back room of the home. We spent many days in the jacuzzi, laughing and joking, mostly just us kids. Adults rarely ever joined us in the jacuzzi, choosing to only be in when we were out or others were around. One night we were in the jacuzzi… me, the guys from next door and my friends. That night one of the adult males decided to join us. It did not seem too strange at first. He allowed us to cuss in front of him and was more of a friend than an authority figure, which was different than most adults we were used to.

He was a masculine guy in his late twenties or early 30s. He looked younger than the other adult choir members. We all sat in the jacuzzi, laughing and joking our normal tween-age banter. I remember he sat across from me as we talked. Each of us sat legs either crossing or linked to the person opposite him. At one point, my foot ended up near his crotch. My foot eventually grazed his penis, and I was stunned. Shocked even more because he looked at me more with a coy smile than disapproval. He closed his leg more in on mine keeping it in place, all this under water. No one except us two knew what was happening. My foot stayed on his penis, now erect.

My friends begin to leave the jacuzzi to head to the living room for snacks and to watch a movie. I sat there not moving…I don't even think I wanted to move or knew how to move. My heart was racing… not fearful… not excited but racing. The room became small, and I was swallowed into what seemed like a scene from a movie. My memory of what happened next is like a filmstrip… images, moments and words. I lost control of me not knowing whether I wanted to or not. In flashes, I remember what happened… with smells and taste imprinted.

When we were alone he reached over slowly and grasped my penis under the water. My heart felt like it was beating outside of my chest. My breathing was so heavy, my chest moved. He whispered for me to stand up and I did. The moments seem like flashes, sitting to standing… not knowing how. He performed oral sex on me. I was overwhelmed by the feeling. There was no sound in the room… quiet. There was no thought that someone might see. I remember thinking, "I just have to keep breathing"… my chest moving up and down.

The memories are like a scene from a Charlie Chaplin film only in color with smells and taste… I try to forget.

Next flash he was standing over me. I sat on the base of the Jacuzzi. It was almost more like I was watching the scene than participating. He motioned me to reciprocate. I tried to oblige I am sure but cannot envision it. I remember his hairy pubic area and the smell. I can still hear him telling me, "Watch your teeth." I remember thinking I was a zombie. My heart racing my eyes wide awake, breathing heavy. I did not know how much time passed…if he ejaculated or when he or I stopped. I do not know how we went from one scene to the next.

Next flash, he sat on a chair outside of the jacuzzi. I stood wrapping a towel around myself. Feeling the urge to get out of the room before I passed out.

He, while lighting a cigarette asked, "Are you going out there like that?" nodding his head toward my crotch.
I looked down to see my penis erect.

I tell him "Yeah", my voice quaking.

I didn't care about anyone seeing in that moment. I was not completely sure of what had just happened. After I wrapped the towel around me, he called me over to him and told me to kiss him. I don't remember taking the steps, but I remember the taste of the cigarette in my mouth. I was a kid…just barely out of puberty.
I walked out to the living room to be with my friends. They all sat watching a movie while our host sat sleeping at the dining room table. All were unaware of what just happened in the other room. I joined them watching the movie…dazed but going through the motions like nothing happened…quietly there but not present. We watched the movie and fell asleep in the living room. Some of us on the floor, side by side… others on couches and chairs. That night I woke up to the adult male beside me. I was lying on my back surprisingly, not the way I normally sleep. He had his hand under my blanket rubbing my privates…I tensed up when I realized what was happening. The fact that my friends laid all around us did not matter to him.

He whispered in my ear, asking if I wanted penetrated sex. I stayed really still…too afraid to move, my heart racing again. He got up and stood over me only wearing a hoody no underwear.

"Come with me upstairs", he whispered.

I laid there not able to move, not even looking around… heart beating rapidly…eyes fixed on him. He gestured for me to come with him. I didn't respond…I could not respond or move. He laid down next to me again. I didn't look over at him...he reached under my cover taking me in his hand and fondled me. He moved his hand. I was sure he was about to get up to try to get me upstairs so I stayed still. Then I felt his mouth on my penis. It didn't last long, I was breathing heavy.

 My eyes were fixed on the ceiling fan. I watched it go around and around…pretending I was not there.
"How does that feel?" he whispered.
I could not respond…I just lay there unable to move. He took my hand placed it on his privates and whispered for me to return the act. My eyes still fixed on the ceiling fan I do not remember moving my hand. I became aware of the people around me. I hoped they were all still sleeping, unaware. I wondered where our host was. Then I heard him still snoring loudly in the dining room. He was asleep at the table. It was not long until he began to breathe heavy and my hand was covered with semen. I don't recall who cleaned it off, just closing my eyes and sleeping.

The next day was like nothing happened. Another morning while there he was taking a shower and ran out of soap. I was told to go up and take it to him while he showered. I opened the door and saw him through the glass shower door. I was not afraid of him. The attention he was now giving me somehow felt okay, I longed for it. I did not necessarily want the acts, but the fact that he desired me…that he touched me made me feel present to someone. This was the first affectionate encounter I had with a man since my father hugged me the night he left…the first of any affection since my mother died. I think a part of me longed for it. The acts in the moment were scary… almost too much for me but a part of me felt like I needed it. In the bathroom, he realized I was there. He told me to kiss him. I did as told, feeling like I would do anything for the attention I was getting.

Later that day he lay in the bedroom upstairs. One of the guys and I went up to look through our host's CD collection to take a few home. My friend left when he found what he wanted leaving me alone with him in the room. He called me to sit on the bed…I shyly made may way to the bed. When I sat down facing the opposite way of him he slipped his hand under me. He began massaging… fondling me. I sat there looking away, scared someone will come in and see. The door of the room was still open. Anyone could walk upstairs and see…he did not seem to care.

He asked me if I would like him to penetrate me, only in more brass language. He told me to stand up and I did. I moved to the corner of the bed and sat up. He then grabbed my crotch and unzipped my pants. The door was still open and he did not seem to care. He performed fellatio on me and I allowed him. My heart racing again. I could not speak, only succumb to the moment. I ejaculated in his mouth and it frightened me. He slapped my butt and smiled wiping his mouth with his shirt and told me to go ahead down stairs. After I ejaculated that first time, I hated him.

In the moments of the acts I had no feeling towards him. I had no thoughts only inner longings to be touched. It wasn't until I saw him a few weeks later that I knew how much I hated him. I felt dirty and ashamed of myself. I was ashamed of what I had done. I was ashamed that I wanted him to touch me again and not just him but anyone. I hated that being touched was all I could think about since that weekend. I masturbated any moment that I could get alone after that. Sex seemed to be all I could think of. I fantasized about sex with teachers and girls in the neighborhood. I became more adamant about having sex with my girlfriends.

I became hyper-sexual. I began a relationship with a woman that lived up the sidewalk from me. She lived on her own and had a son. A couple of my friends and I had girlfriends who were older. This woman and I had the biggest age gap. Although I was only a teen, still in middle school, she and I began a sexual relationship. Not only was I having sex with her but also a girl my own age that I was also dating. To me it had little to do with the person I was having sex with or the climax.

I would spend many days with the older woman. Some nights she would buy alcohol…my friends and I would hangout at her place. We would play card games and chill, pretending we were adults too. Once we tricked my middle school secretary by calling the older woman so she could get me out of school early to spend the day with her. Our relationship was short-lived and my aunt was not in approval. She eventually moved away, yet we stayed friends.

Fear Love

We are lost and some of us can't find our way
Pain clouds the way, blinds us
Never thinking words could cut so deep
Was I not your son?
Did you not once hold me in your arms?
Was I not once yours and known by you?
Yet with every drunken slap you broke me
A father is supposed to protect but you beat me instead and I fear
you, Still.
Bruises you said you did cause you love me…
Could I change the way I talk or my mannerisms?
Should I wipe away all that was in me as I tried and wished?
And as you tried to beat it out me you broke me
"Faggot" not in my house, he screams!
My friend, I knew not a man nor did I wish it too
Dance was just a part of me
Artist is who I am meant to be
He couldn't understand me
So he tried to rid me of what he couldn't understand
Trying to beat what he thought I was out of me
Not knowing he was damaging me
And now I cant hold you any closer
My trepidation being I might break you
Close but not too, near but not enough to be vulnerable

Scream! Cry for us. Write for us my friend
Its been to long and still no one will sing our song
Quiet. Shame too damn loud
It's in the room no will acknowledge, see me!
Look past the shell of the man you think you see
Because we Broken Boys have become wounded men
Who fear Love, cause we hide scars silence wont let heal…

Chapter Seven
In Pieces

Who Hate

We Broken Boys
Molested by those who should have protected
By Priest and Preachers, Neighbors and Teachers
Stealing from us every ounce of innocence
No one speaks our silence
Cause we don't have wombs we carry no emotion?
Were we not your children?
With every touch they leave us...Broken.
Confused. Longing to be touched.
Thinking this just may be love.
Made to touch places only your wife should
You touching me, whispers, "Don't that feel good?"
You are breaking me
You sucking, me silent
Stunned. Unable to move
You play with my... You just going to stick the head in
You are breaking me, this hurts me
And I like shattered glass, window broken
No protection, entry
Like rain, floods me
Dark Pain
Lonely making me despise all that I am
Write my friend, speak for us...

Did I deserve this?
How did I cause it?
Dirt on me I can't wash away, get it off me!
Am I nasty?
Unwanted?
Do you see it on me?
Can you tell?
Do you know what he did?
Can you see?
We Broken Boys have become Wounded men
Who hate ourselves, because we hide scars silence won't let heal...

After seeing someone murdered, I hated the way of life in the projects. I began to escape into books. At my aunt's house, I became more and more reclusive. My friends and I had begun to take different directions in life. Our only real connection was our singing group. My uncle on my father's side bought my paternal grandmother, Granny Gail, a house. The house was across the street from the housing projects. Though it was just a few blocks away from where I lived it seemed to be whole different world. The house represented a whole new life. For me, it was my way out.

I began living with my grandmother what would have been the fall of my eighth grade year…had I not been expelled from school. I had to do seventh grade twice since I was suspended so much. When I finally reached eighth grade, I was expelled after only a couple months. My former seventh grade teacher reported that he felt threatened by me, leading to a school board hearing where they finally expelled me.

The move into my grandmother's house was gradual. I began spending more and more time there with my cousin Vanessa. She was a little younger than me and my grandmother had taken her in. Her mom was my aunt, the sister of my grandmother. She was serving time in prison. My aunt had another daughter who lived in a foster home at that time.

After weeks of spending night after night there, I finally called it home. Vanessa's mom eventually was released, and she moved back in with her. When Vanessa moved out, two of my other cousins moved in, Mannie and Lil Charles. We were like brothers. My grandmother spoiled each of us individually. I received more of her attention and affection. She justified her favoritism of me because I was her eldest grandchild and didn't have a mother. The times that we shared together in that house I still hold dear to my heart. Some are great memories…others I wish I could forget.

My grandmother had always been the one I counted on, my constant.

Anytime I needed anything or to get out of anything, she was the one I would call. My grandma had been with my step-grandfather Big Paul since my dad was a kid. He died the year I officially moved in. When I made her place home, I took over the space. I had my own room, and my cousins shared one. My grandmother was also taking care of her mother Granny Vera at the time. Granny Vera, my great-grandmother, was sick and suffering from some memory loss. She would sometimes use her memory loss against us. Granny Vera was weak and would not try to walk as her nurse asked. She smoked all of my life, but when she moved in with us my grandmother would not allow her to smoke unless she ate or tried to walk for exercise.

A fond memory of her is of one particular evening she wanted a cigarette. She tried to convince one of us kids to bring her one. She was not willing to try to walk, telling the nurse she couldn't do it that day. We did not succumb to her cries for a cigarette, knowing she was not allowed to have one. She sat in her room alone watching TV with the door shut this evening. My grandmother was out, and I was alone there with my cousins.

After a while I heard commotion coming from the room. When I walked to open the door I found her standing at the dresser. She was moving things around looking for her pack of cigarettes. I called out to her and asked what she was doing. She was startled that she was busted. When she realized she was busted the trickery began. She stretched out her hands and pretended to be disoriented. She asked me how she got there. When I told her she knew what she was doing she, half-laughing but trying to maintain her serious composure, asked, "Can I have a cigarette?" This was the first of many of these hilarious episodes.

Granny Vera lived with us a while in Nashville. We would often take trips to Celina to her trailer to stay weekends and summers. We spent most of the year before I started High School in the country. My grandmother became addicted to prescription drugs in this time. We were unaware that she was addicted until years down the line.

She complained of pain in her legs…a pain that would leave her unable to function. She did whatever she could to buy Tylenols 3's, Valiums, or whatever drugs were the strongest to soothe her. After taking the drugs she would lay on the couch with a glazed look in her eyes, often with a Blow Pop or some sweet in her mouth. I think it just became normal to us. We didn't think much of it. It often provided an easy way to get our way. It wasn't until years later that she finally acknowledged that it was not actual pain she was feeling in her legs but something she had conjured up in her mind out of need for her drugs.

My grandmother stood about five-eight and weighs about one-hundred pounds. Although she was a skinny lady, she was one not to be messed with. She was the family's matriarch. The entire family revolved around her and our house. It was a lively place. Every day there would always be something happening. Granny Gail would host card games at her house with her friends. They would play spades long into the morning hours...a group, mostly ladies, gambling for big money…sitting around the table each of them with their purses in the laps. Most carried a pistol or some weapon in case something went wrong.

My grandmother was known to a lot of my friends as "Gangsta Granny." She was as sweet as any grandmother I knew. She always made sure we had food to eat. She was the best cook I know and took good care of her family. On the flip side of her abilities to mother she also served as an in-between for a lot of the drug dealing in my family. I recall countless calls of her getting orders for some type of drugs over the phone. She would use cooking terms to differentiate the type of drugs and the amount. For instance, for marijuana she would use turnip green and bushels to determine the amount.

I remember once, visitors came into town to acquire drugs from a deal that was set up. Apparently, before the transaction could occur, someone had stolen money from my uncle, her brother. I sat on the couch watching TV with the remote in hand and my little cousins beside me. I was not really paying attention. I was lost in the show I was watching. I finally became aware that the visitors were disturbed by what was happening.

The night was like a scene from a comedy sitcom. The men kept relaying to her that they had no idea what happened. One of the guys was about six-three, weighing at least three hundred pounds, the other smaller in stature and older. They both sat on couches opposite me. When my grandmother couldn't get an answer from them as to where the missing money was she said, in her signature words, "Well, I'll tell you what." She went back to her room, grabbed a shotgun, and pointed it in their direction. This sent both of them into a fright.

I nonchalantly told my little cousins to go back into my room to watch TV. I sat flicking the channels like the episode in real life was not happening. This had become my new normal life. One of my other uncles came in, took the gun from her and she went to get another one. This happened twice and then somehow he helped to settle the situation as I sat unshaken, watching TV. I do not know if they found out what happened with the missing money or not.

I spent that summer in Celina as normal. It was then that I truly knew that behind the picture painted of family and fun lay secrets that as a child I was not privy to…drug deals that went on right before our faces…with us unaware…trips taken back and forth carrying drugs that we had no idea were with us. I wasn't aware until my late teen years just how deep my family was in the drug business. By then it was normal life…a life that would, in years to come, be shattered by the arrest of a great deal of my father's family.

I always knew my family was involved somewhat in drugs, and the life that we led there provided great comfort. We had workers that cleaned and took care of the house. Mostly drug users who were paid in drugs or enough money to get them high. Those people were more than junkies or drug users to us they were extensions of our family. They cooked for us, when my grandmother didn't feel like it, made our beds, did the laundry. At times they even drove us back and forth to school or wherever we would like to go. This was the life I was used to living with my grandmother.

When I finally went back to school after being expelled they moved me up to the ninth grade. The life I had lived in that past year had impacted me greatly…from meeting "The Preacher" to my new way of life with my Dad's family. I had always been conscious of how I dressed, but for me now, not only how I looked but what brands I wore became very important. During those times I would buy a new pair of shoes almost weekly. My clothes all had to be the same name brand, including socks and underwear. I was losing me in the lifestyle.

At home my change became evident. My uncle would say to me, "Boy, you got them people thinking you live in Brentwood." Brentwood was a more affluent area on the outskirts of Nashville. My friends were a mixed group more White and Asian. My uncle was my only rival of my dad's siblings. I think it was because of the way my grandmother treated me. All the siblings, including my dad, would say, "You never treated us like you treat them." As long as grandmother was around, my cousins and I could get away with just about anything.

The life that we lived seemed glorious on the outside but at times was also strenuous on us kids. At one point underneath my bed were hidden pump action shotguns with infrared beams. I remember countless times coming home to my uncles in the kitchen, which was near my room, preparing drugs or counting large amounts money.

There was one day after coming home from school, I walked into the house to what seemed to be a normal day. I got to my room and noticed that my bed was completely broken down. My drawers were all across my room and the contents on the floor. I was confused. I turned around immediately and went into the living room to ask my family. I asked what happened to my room. There sitting in the living room was my grandmother, my Uncle Calvin and my ten year old cousin, Mannie.

My grandmother then told me that the cops raided the place earlier that morning and that Donna, our housekeeper, would clean my room later. By then the event had become old news to them. My cousin Mannie looked at me with eyes wide open. I could tell by the look he wanted to share more. My cousin told me a little later his account of the story. He shared the fear of so many men busting into the house with guns. He was confused as the men were not all dressed like police officers. As they rushed in and started hurling questions he stood in fear with his hands raised. He told me he said to the officer, as they burst into the door, "All I know is I missed the bus and I couldn't go to school." We busted into laughter at the statement. We learned to find laughter no matter what the situation.

There were also times that we felt terrified of what we were so closely attached to…times when white men followed us in cars as we walked from our school buses…nights of fear that someone would break in assuming that money was in the home. I remember one night sitting in the house alone, I got a call from my grandmother telling me someone is going to bring some money that I needed to sit on. Not long after that a guy knocks on the door and asked if my uncle was around. I told him no but he could leave it with me.

The guy was someone I recognized from our neighborhood, not much older than me. He handed me a package of what I would eventually find out to be several thousands of dollars. I was to put the money under the couch cushion and sit there until my uncle came. I remember sitting there on the couch on top of the money and looking at the door. Any sound sent my heart beating rapidly. I sat praying that he would hurry and come.

My grandmother's house was quite different from the lifestyle I had known as a young child. It felt like home. I'd always known how much my grandmother cared for me. Even while my mother was alive I knew I was special to her. I do not think I ever knew I was special to anyone after my mom's death, other than by her. To her I was an angel, even though I was far from one. I always knew she would defend me, protect me. I would always tell my friends, "If no one else cares about me, my grandmother does." Her love for me spilled into all those who were close to me...my friends and even those who were not related to her would call her Granny Gail. She took the place of my mother, although we were not affectionate at all in the family. There were still no hugs or I love you's. Affection was shown in gifts and money.

Though she was my dad's mom, not much changed in me and my dads relationship. My dad would still come to make his occasional visits. He came to stay for two visits with us that were the most memorable. One was right before Christmas one year. He had come to see us in hopes of taking me back to spend the holidays with him. During the visit, two of my younger cousins began arguing, which was a normal occurrence. When he came in and found that they were still arguing, a scene that we were accustomed to, he was irate with me. He was upset that I would allow them to argue.

For the first time in my life I stood up to him. I was fifteen years old, and it surprised us both. I never talked back to my dad, but I think the frustration over the years had built to its breaking point. I also had an assurance that he could not harm me because he feared my grandmother. Initially, I think shock overtook him, he then grabbed me by my shirt. He tried to pull me to the back room of the house, where he planned on whooping me. At fifteen I think I made up my mind that I was too old for a whooping, especially by him. So in my anger I pushed him off me, nearly off the back patio of the house.

He was nearly ready to fight. Instead of retaliating, he walked away, steaming in anger. He left the house. He went to go get a drink with his friend. When he left I got dressed for the day. After I stood in the doorway between the living room and my room brushing my hair, my aunt asked me where I was going. She asked with a coy smile because apparently I had put on something really nice. I replied matter-of-factly, "to jail."

She busted into laughter, almost uncontrollably. She wanted to know why I was going to jail. I told her I was going to kill my father. Still laughing she asked me how. She laughed so hard tears were streaming down her face. She was amused at my candor and how nonchalant I was. I told her that I was going to shoot my dad with my grandmother's 38 in her drawer. I went to retrieve the gun to show her.

When I brought the gun back she laughed even more heartily. Through her tears and laughter she told me the gun was broken. At this we both laughed. My father came back and apologized for what happened. He was near drunk. All was forgiven, but I chose not to go to Indiana with him. That year for Christmas he gave me a Rottweiler puppy and a broken camcorder. I named the puppy Mannie, after my little cousin.

Another visit was a few years later. It was one of my Dad's attempts to live in Nashville. Although this exploit was short-lived, it was quite vivid to me. He initially stayed with us at my grandmother's. Early one morning around 5:30, he tried to wake me before he went to work so I could get ready for school. I sheepishly told him I was not waking up that early for school. We argued back and forth him trying to show his authority, me arguing that those rights were relinquished when he left me as a child. I had become extremely bitter towards him. I talked to him in a way that I did not talk to anyone, especially not adults.

I turned on the movie "The Color Purple" as I always did before and after school. I was letting him know he had no control and I was going to do what I wanted.

The argument ended with him screaming, "Boy, I'm YOUR daddy!

Get up! Get dressed!."
I retorted in my anger, "My dad is in the other room."

I was referring to my grandmother laying in the room down the hall. I then began to call "Daddy! Daddy," to my grandmother who listened but did not intervene. He left the house that day and did not sleep there again. I harbored a lot of hate against my dad for many years. My disrespect and blatant disregard for his feelings were a result of that…something I'm not proud of.

I still went to church every Sunday while living with my grandmother. Even when we were in Celina, my grandmother would make sure I could get back to be at church on Sunday. They had no idea about what happened in the jacuzzi. I put that in a different box in my mind…I lived like it did not exist. I wondered if they knew at times. I suspected my grandmother had questions and concerns about me when she met "The Preacher."

Who Hide

We feel alone…
In a world that wont accept our confusion
In churches who won't embrace our mess as truth
My friend, write that we hide behind suits, ties and titles
Feign wholeness and suffer for it
And underneath the picture we have painted lies a canvas
White with fear and desperation
Hoping that someone will see that once we were clean
Once we could feel and we felt loved
But not any more because we 'do it' to be touched.
To be held. To feel wanted.
Hoping that what we have sacrificed will be enough,
We long to feel again.
And so many sit in judgment
Am I not your brother?
Are we not your kin?
Did we not once share and have in common?
Have you forgotten me?
Look at us my friend, Scream for us

We your husbands and lovers
With issues that spill into everything we do
You confide in us not knowing that our strength is our weakness
We like stone pillars you lean on crumble within from hurts from
our past, Silent.
Silence you call strength and it is raping me all over again
I can't take it anymore
I cannot be quiet, it hurts me!

The mess of a man you see today was once a boy
Unprotected. Raped or Molested. Beaten or Rejected
Feeling unloved. Unaccepted.
Were we not your brothers?
Did you not once walk with us.

Now we stand before you ashamed of ourselves
Ashamed of what he did to us.
Broken by how she beat us
Wounded by unreturned love.

My friend write. Scream. Cry.
We Broken Boys have become Wounded Men
Who hide behind mask cause we hide scars silence won't let heal!

Chapter Eight
The Preacher

Preacher

I was spread like cloth on altar
Sacrifice
I almost lost me
In lust and deception
He came, Told me all I had ever done
Like psychic, I thought
Told me my heart and its secrets
My future and past
Prophecy
I admired him for his gift
And I almost gave all of me away
Like bread taken and broken for men
Brother was like sheep and wolf
Peace and wrath
Told me God sent him to help me
He like Moses calling Joshua, I thought
The girls at church look at him like lions on prey
He looked at me the same way, only I lay unaware
He told me all I had ever done and I trusted
Prophet and Pastor
And I almost lost me, me
In lies and false tales
My second time was with oil
From which he laid hands with on Sunday
Whispers in my ear
Our secret
Sleepovers
Special times in his office
And he laid me, like linen on the communion table
Offering
Spread me like woman
I gave in, I trusted
Him Climaxing

Me, panting and deep breathing
Pain feeling like He is ripping me apart
And I let it happened stunned
As his friends watched
I remember it like flashes
Old movie on strips
I trusted
I almost lost me
In words and hopes, aspirations of a God-man
I was 15 years old my second time
He told me all that I had ever done
Told me I would be like him one day, a Preacher

Although I stayed with my dad's family, who never attended church, church was still a constant in my life. It was there that I would have another encounter that would impact my life tremendously. He walked into the church and every female under sixty stared him down, the older ones cutting their eyes. It was an Easter Sunday I was fourteen, turning fifteen that year. The church was pretty packed. Most of those attending, we had not seen since last Easter. When the time for altar call came the gentleman was asked to lead the congregation in prayer.

The congregation sang "Pray for Me," in preparation for the prayer to come…a song that had become a prayer in itself. He made his way to the podium and the women sneaked peeps at him. He was an attractive light-skinned guy. He stood about 5'10 with a short clean haircut. He wore a nice suit and tie that made him look very distinguished. He began to pray and his accent had everyone peeking up to make sure he was the same man called up to pray. No one expected the Bahamian inflections. His prayer was powerful and passionate. The older women in the church yelled and moaned as he prayed. There were only about three adult males, besides the ministers.

I was later introduced to the gentleman who had made the memorable introduction in the pulpit. He was from the Bahamas and a student at one of the predominantly black Baptist college in Nashville. Our pastor at that time was also a student at the same college. The Pastor told him that I was singing with a well-known choir around town, while giving me warning about the notorious reputation of the choir director. I was fifteen years old and had begun to rehearse with another well-known choir in town. He also made him aware that I was expelled from school for the remainder of the year.

When the Pastor walked away The Preacher told me that he was also a student at a University about 30 minutes outside of Nashville. I was impressed to hear he was a student at two colleges. Where I came from, to see a black man in any school after eighteen was impressive. The Preacher was well spoken and every teenaged girl in the building found an excuse to stop by the Pastor's office to get another look at him. He was in his early twenties and a psychology major at the university while studying theology at the Baptist College. He told me he was taking a psychology class at the university that required him to bring in a youth for discussion. He then asked me if I would like to go with him and be a part of the project since I was expelled and did not have school. I agreed, and he gave me his number and told me to call him later that evening to make plans.

That night I called as I was asked. I remember being unusually nervous as the phone rang. I have never been a fan of talking to other guys on the phone. He answered, and we spoke a little, making plans for me to go to the university with him. He told me we would be there for a while and I could bring shorts to swim at the university's recreation center. In the class we would attend, each of the students was to bring a child with them to participate in the class discussion. Later in the conversation he asked me if I was okay, if anything was going on in my life. The question surprised me. I wondered if I led on like something was wrong, if anything had been evident in my voice.

He then began to tell me what was going on with me…prophesying about my current situation. He told me exactly what was going on in my heart. He knew things I had not shared with anyone…my girlfriend was moving away in a couple of days. He knew it, and how I felt about it. He expressed my care for her and that I did not want her to move away. I was astounded at what he knew. As we talked, I paced my room on the corded phone at my grandmother's house.

I asked him how he knew what he disclosed to me. He told me it was part of his gifting. If any guards were up, they all went down after that. From then on I became an open book to him. The rest of the conversation that night was me telling him how I felt about my girlfriend moving away, an instant trust was made. I shared with him things I never shared with anyone. I even told him about having sex with her and the older women in the neighborhood. All my guards were down with him.

The day he came to pick me up was one of mixed emotions…the excitement of doing something other than lying around the house and the fight to believe he was going to come like he said he would. When he arrived that spring day we sat on my grandmother's porch. He walked up and introduced himself to her. Her reaction to him surprised me. She seemed to question his motives. Her mannerisms were almost defensive in nature. I watched, bewildered at their interaction. She allowed us to go, almost reluctantly.

He had two friends with him that day that were visiting from the Bahamas. They did not get out of the car with him to come to the porch. When we got to the car they sat in the backseat. He introduced us. I coyly greeted the guys, feeling intimidated by their presence. We stopped at a restaurant for lunch where I got to know the guys a little better. One was a slim guy, my complexion and well put together. He was noticeably more feminine but I did not think much of it. Growing up in the church music world feminine guys were normal. The other was a thicker guy with dark skin. He was more masculine and quiet. They had grown up with The Preacher in the Bahamas. After lunch we made our way to the class, which was not that memorable. I sat along with other kids mostly white, some younger.. some older. We were asked questions about something or other and we answered. While The Preacher and I were in class his friends walked the campus of the university.

After the class ended we met up with his friends and went to the recreational center to swim. I forgot to bring a suit, but he had an extra one there for me. His friends, for reasons I do not remember, did not swim. In the pool, The Preacher and I played games and raced while his friends watched from the side. Our games became a wrestling match for a ball we played with in the pool. What seemed to be a normal time of playing quickly escalated into something different. As we wrestled we grabbed each other trying take the ball from the other. His grabbing became more towards my groin. Adrenaline began to surge through my body.

I was surprised that it was happening but just thought it to be my imagination initially. I remember thinking, "What would his friends say if they saw what was going on?" The more we wrestled, the more he made sure to grab me in a way that would expose his penis to me. Finally, he grabbed me from behind gripping me tightly. I could feel his privates against me. By then he was erect. My heart raced, and I was confused. Was this the same guy who on phone last night told me what only God knew? I thought maybe my mind was playing tricks on me. The game began to intensify with him, making sure that I knew he was turned on.

We continued fighting for the ball. Finally, he held me again in a position with his privates to my backside. It was then evident and undeniable what was happening. He whispered for me to come with him. He adjusted his shorts and beckoned me to follow him, and I did. I did not think of what would happen if I followed. I did not think of where we would go. There was no thought that my going with him would lead to anything. I just went. We went into the locker room first. As I followed he looked around making sure no ones else was there. He quickly led me into a shower stall. He closed the curtain quickly behind us.

Time flashed again the same kind of flashing I experienced not so long ago…in and out of reality scared…too breathe scared to move. He grabbed me tightly and kissed me aggressively. It seemed like I was both there and gone. I remember at one point thinking of my great grandmother, Lizbeth. It was like I was slipping in and out of the moment…flashes of him performing oral sex on me.

Memories of the song "Amazing Grace" playing in my head. I doubt if he even recognized I was not fully there. The next flash he ejaculates in the shower. I stood…not moving, not touching me or

94

him, just still. He again aggressively kisses me and leaves the stall. I stood there not moving, ashamed to open the curtains or to even breathe loudly. I stood ashamed and bewildered. It seemed like I had been in the shower standing for hours when The Preacher peeked his head in and asked me if I was okay. I gave no answer, just looked... acknowledging his presence. I do not remember thinking at the time...just standing.

When he returned I tried to reconcile in my mind what had transpired. He told me he had my clothes ready for me. I wrapped the towel around myself. His friends were waiting in the locker room near our locker. The dazed feeling I had must have been evident to them, yet they sat on benches waiting for me to change. I was more ashamed than ever. I was hesitant to take off my shorts off in front of them. I felt like I was already naked before them. I wondered if they knew what had happened. My behavior must have been apparent, he asked them leave me alone to dress. They obliged.

As I dressed he told me that they would drop me off at home a little later. He spoke with me like nothing happened. I dressed quietly, still trying to wrap my head around it all. The sitting arrangement on the way home changed. The masculine friend moved to the driver's seat and the other took my seat in the front. The Preacher and I sat in the back seat. On the way he held my hand in the back seat under the radar of his mates in the front. He then began to grope me. My body became tense, wondering if they could see what he was doing. He began kissing me aggressively again in the backseat. It was then I knew that his friends were aware of what was happening. I wondered if they knew what happened in the shower.

After that day he began to pick me up every few days for the next few weeks...sometimes early in the morning, telling my guardians I was going to the university with him to the course again. He paid a great deal of attention to me. I was not used to the treatment he gave me. While his friends were still visiting, we went to see a Gospel play at the World Baptist Center. As we sat watching the play he held my hand. I was shocked by it, wondering if anyone would see. During the intermission of the play we went out to the church van we had ridden to the play in. While his friends stood on the outside of the van we had our second sexual encounter. I remember being terrified someone would see, he seemed not to care.

Another night we picked up some of the other youth from the church to attend an event. I remembered the girls talking about how handsome he was. Some even flirted with him, hoping to win his attention. After the event he dropped the others off. He saved me for the last stop. As we rode he asked me questions about my other sexual experiences. He wondered if I had ever been with another man. I told him about the jacuzzi event. The event seemed to turn him on. He asked me if the guy from the jacuzzi penetrated me. I did not know what the word meant.

He explained to me what it meant to be penetrated. I had never thought of that kind of sex. It was new to me. He told me he enjoyed to bottom. He asked me what I preferred, top or bottom. I told him I did not know. The terms were new to me. Most of what I would experience with him was new to me. He told me he wanted to be my first. One of the morning pick-ups he took me back to his apartment where he had prepared breakfast. While I sat at the table eating he showered and went to the bedroom. He called me in where he was already naked. It was there we had penetrated sex.

After sex he seemed to be angry with me. He accused me of having sex with him like he was a woman, a concept that I did not fully understand. I had only had penetrated sex with women. The anger subsided as he became himself again. This anger or frustration with me would show up now and then often after sex. The anger was really his shame being projected onto me. One day in anger he told me not to judge him because I would be a preacher like him someday.

I did not mind having sex with him. I thrived on the attention he gave me. Some days before sex, he would take me out. We would go to an expensive restaurant in town that I had never heard of. Some places he would order for me because I had no idea how to pronounce things on the menu. He would use valet parking instead of parking the car himself. The restaurants would give you bread you dipped in oil, a completely new concept to me then. Here I was not an inner city kid… I was special. He treated me like I was special to him.

In those days pagers were all the rage. We stayed connected in the little time we spent together. His code in my pager was 919, a code that was used in the Bahamas. After meals or events we would try different things. I had never felt the way he treated me. As the weeks passed he became more adventurous with me. He took me to the park one day and told me about men having sex there secretly. Things I was not aware of as kid. He wanted to have sex in the park too and then in the car as he drove. He made me feel cared for.

One day as I sat at my aunt's house I received a page from him. He was at the church alone painting. He wanted me to come to the church to see him there. He always made me feel like I was the most important thing in the world to him. The thirst in me to feel like I was somebody's must have been strong. The desire to have someone, a man, make you feel like you are a part of him must have been discernible. I was thirsty to belong to someone. As perverse as it was, he became a temporary filler for the longings. I would do whatever he asked.

The day he was at the church I rushed to meet him. When I got there it was just he and I alone. As soon as the door was locked behind me he near pounced on me, kissing and groping. I was freaked out by the fact we were in the church. He pulled me into the Pastor's office. My mind was trying to wrap around being there and doing what we were doing. This was the same church I sang in Sunday after Sunday…the same place where years earlier I mourned my mother.

This building had once been a safe place.

The Preacher was aggressive as always in sexual encounters. He grabbed me, and I pulled away this time telling him we should not do it here. There was no care that we were in the church. Leaning on the Pastor's desk he pulled down his pants. Grabbing me from behind he pulled down my pants. I gave into the moment. He penetrated me forcefully. I, at first, tried to get him to stop telling him it hurt but he trying to calm me told me to just relax. I do not remember if it lasted long or not. I seemed to have blacked out. This was a first for me, and it was painful.

The place that had for many years been a hiding place had been perverted. I remember him pulling up his pants and telling me I needed to leave before the Pastor came back. The pastor had told me not to hang with The Preacher alone or without his knowledge. A warning I thought was not needed so I did not heed it. When I pulled up my pants I felt his semen in and around my anus. I didn't wash myself I pulled my pants up and left the church.

I walked to my aunt's house. As I walked I still felt the pain of him being in me. I wondered on that walk if anyone could tell what I had just done. It was a walk of shame through my community. Sex was no more flashes of moments. I was aware of what was going on. I had begun to take part it in. I was getting the attention and affection I longed for. It was not until after the sex was over that the shame and hate came. It always came after without fail.

A few days later The Preacher told me he was engaged to a woman. He told me he was moving away soon. He also told me not to judge him, saying I would be like him one day, a preacher. We spent a few more days together. Sexual encounters in his home, car or in some parking lot. After every encounter he began telling me how much he was in love with me. I was fifteen and believed him. I was in love with idea that someone loved me. I don't remember enjoying any of the sex, but I was enthralled by the attention. He eventually moved away, and I moved on with a new feeling of what love was. Love had become sex, and I would do anything to feel loved again. I was enthralled with being touched by people, male or female to me there was no difference. It was not based on attraction but a longing that needed to be filled. I became very promiscuous.

Shame

You wear it like cloak
It covers like warmth only unwanted
Waking with you
Like light only dark
It causes you to despise all you are
Like stain on white sheets
Exposing you, to yourself

You wear it like shoes
It's with you throughout the day
Wondering if others can see
You feel it like pain
Guilt and sorrow
It marks you like dirt
Ruining all that you hold
Leaving you unwanted, to yourself

You wear it like a coat
Sliding into it arm by arm
It engulfs you, swallows you up
You know it like self
You hate it just the same
It causes you to give into it
Leads you too sadness
Calls you from regret
Abandoning you, to yourself

Chapter Nine
High School Was No Musical

Dance

Music and Tone, Expression
Focus is in the gaze of the eyes, even in dance
Internally; aware of sensations in the body
External; full attention to the space outside the body
Let go. Be Present. Fully Aware.
They say I move like wind, painting earth's face with leaves, like
Autumn
Sometimes dance is all you got, give yourself to it.
Dance
Verb meaning to move rhythmically to music
Typically following a set sequence of steps
Terpsichorean
Practice, rehearse, train, teach the body
Some movements I learned while dodging his hits
They say I flow like water, rain on dry ground
Yielding life, like Spring
Isn't it funny how someone who dances like water can feel like rock
on the inside
You give yourself to it
Let go, it holds you and nothing else exist outside it
Arabesque
Body becomes like mold. Memory. Kinesthetic.
They say I move like Spirit and Sound chasing unseen harm away
Form and Pose, Turns and Positions, Rise and Fall
Dance
Like Life choreographed in Fear and Love
Different yet perceived the same
Like Father and Son
Fist and Love
Dance like Wind moving.
Water Flowing. Spirit and Sound.
Sometimes it's all you got.
And you give yourself to it
Dance

When I was finally allowed to go back to school I was moved up to high school…moved simply due to my age. When I started high school I was elated to join the Half-timers squad. Half-timers was the school dance team. The team normally performed during the half-time of basketball games. However, most of us wanted to dance in competitions. The competitions were called "Battle of The Half-timers." Neighboring high schools, predominately African-American, competed.

Our school was mixed, but African-Americans were dominant. A lot of the students were bused in from where I grew up…both from the White and Colored Projects. The other part of our school was students from closer to the school.

My friends and I had talked for years about the opportunity to dance in high school. I jumped at the opportunity to audition without question. I was not alone in my pursuit of becoming a half-timer, my closest friends all tried out.

The tryouts were tedious, but we made it through. I was officially a McGavock Half-timer. Dance consumed most of my time and thoughts. Dance was all I knew outside of music in high school. Over the course of my freshman year my dance teammates and I became close. We would find teen clubs to dance at during the week. We would go anywhere that would house a big group of people to dance. I started branching out to different groups of people that were not from my neighborhood.

During the battle competitions, teams would go all out to win. That year Dru Hill released their first album. They took TV and radio by storm with their style and sound. Often in battles, teams would mix the look of top artists into their routines. I portrayed Sisqó, Dru Hill's lead singer for one of our routines. I became a dancer in that season. I had my uncle cut the words "Freaky J" in my hair for a competition. In these years I did not care what anyone thought of me. I took on the persona completely…I was dance.

I bleached my hair platinum blonde. My inner circle had changed to a group of guys who were as wild as I was in that time. The guys were all very sexual and experimental. None of us really had any idea who we were or how we identified. We were just open to whatever life brought. If we weren't dancing we were figuring out some way to do something sexual.

Although I was dating girls, I was open to nearly anything sexual. We were extremely experimental. My life as a high school student was pretty abnormal compared to others. My friends and I often hung outside the adult bookstore...sometimes we would be allowed inside. Most nights after dancing at the teen club we would spend time outside the bookstore talking and meeting people. Adults would come and have conversations with us and not even question our age or the appropriateness of even being in such a place.

The adult bookstore was a place full of characters. The people that entered and left amused us. Around the bookstore were male prostitutes. Occasionally, my friends and I would solicit one while others watched on. Sex had to come with a thrill. We were all between the ages of fifteen and seventeen. I was a different person, no longer the quiet book reader. I never felt so open to try anything without caring if I would be judged. Sex was common and expected in my inner circle. Everyone wanted sex and older men wanted it from us.

The summer before high school I met an older guy. I was at a swimming pool that my friends and I frequented. We met in the steam room and the sexual episodes began. They continued into high school. One evening while going out with him we ran into trouble. We were busted by the cops. We were supposed to be headed to another high school's talent show. Instead of heading there, we made a detour to a park. By then I had become good at getting out of the house to do what I wanted without question. My grandmother trusted me.

At the park our behavior became sexual in nature. Lost in the moment we were unaware of our surroundings…the song "Stairway to Heaven" playing in the background. We were completely oblivious to anything but ourselves until being startled by bright lights. The reality of the situation finally hit us. The bright lights were from the cop car. The lights illuminated the entire car. The guy I was with was an adult, and I was still fifteen…underage. He whispered to me, "Pull your pants up." By then it was too late. The cops were at the window. My heart sank into my stomach.

The cops stood on either side of the car with their flashlights pointed into the window. They put us both into the back seat of their police car. While in the back seat I became hysterical. I begged the officer for his gun.

"Please! Kill me! Just give me your gun and let me kill myself! I might as well die!" I pleaded.
The thought of my family finding out about me being with a guy mortified me. I did not fear they would not accept me but being thought of as gay. It was just sex to me. I never thought of myself as homosexual. To me, I was just scratching an inner itch.

I continued to plead with the cop to just kill me or let me kill myself. My older counterpart pleaded with me to please be quiet. He was distraught himself. They gave him a citation, and hauled me off to juvenile. I guess for boys the term statutory rape has less meaning. While in juvenile detention center, I was finally asked by the officers doing my paperwork if the man I was with was taking advantage me. I told them he was not. There were two officers a male and a female, and they seemed more amused by the situation than concerned.

While processing me, I expressed to them that I did not want my family to find out. I asked it they could keep me locked up forever. The officer told me I would be charged with indecent exposure. The male officer said I could just tell my parents I was peeing in the park. The female agreed, and I did just that. They wanted to help me protect my secret. As I look back on it today I wonder how it would have ended if we had uncovered it…if maybe it would have been better to have protected my childhood instead of saving my secret. However, in that moment, I was relieved to see that there was a way out…even though now, as I write, I am saddened. As a child, those meant to protect me didn't. I think because boys are male we give them responsibility of being grown before their time. We're less likely to protect them…to shield them…to guard their innocence. For me, this wasn't the first time someone didn't speak up for me. I think of the time in the jacuzzi… no adults were around or the time with the Preacher when my pastor didn't speak up against what he thought was happening.

I think we grow so accustomed to protecting our little girls that we push our boys to the wayside. They get ravaged by the wolves. When I was younger, I thought I was just making choices. I thought I was capable of deciding for myself and for my body what was right. But as a man, now I wish that somebody would have spoken up for me. I wish that those officers would have told the truth and that I would have been confronted with what I was doing. I wish my family would have been more concerned with what was going on in my life…that I had my father there to guide me or to shield my heart. That was not my reality.

I got off that evening by excusing the event as an innocent pee in the park. This was not the end of my sexual exploits. By then I was becoming accustomed to dating people older than me. I think after losing my mom, I was perceived to be a lot more mature than my age. My inner circle in school was seen the same way. Though unspoken and not talked about we all yearned to be touched. We all were thirsty. We found ways to try and quench our thirst.

The sex was the height but after came sadness. I hated the person I was becoming but loved the attention I got from it. I thought about killing myself often. I wrote suicide letters apologizing to my cousins and sisters. Sometimes I would write a will leaving my clothes to Mannie and Lil Charles. I would apologize to my sisters for not being able to be strong enough for them. I rarely ever saw them after I moved with my grandmother. After I wrote I would talk myself out of dying. Reasoning I could not put my family through the grief I carried.

High school went by like a flash. I only completed one full year of classes. My freshman year I thrived only to maintain a position on the dance team. As the other years passed I still danced but my involvement in class work was beyond lax. By my third year I was coming to school when I felt like it. The truancy officers visited our home a few times warning me about missing school. I came to school some days at fourth or fifth period and stayed through dance practice. School was not a place for me to learn…just a place to hang out.

It was filled with diverse sexual exploits for me, offers from girls and guys alike. I seemed to be a magnet for sex. Men began hitting on me in the Sunday evening church services I used to escape in. Adult bookstores, threesomes, and dance were my life outside of church. School only played in the background. My life spiraled completely out of control. My sexual partners were not connections just opportunities to try and feel. I could not feel anything. There was never any emotion attached to encounters…just opportunities to believe I was wanted.

The first time I felt for a person was unexpected. It was in 6th period…my Home Economic class. I had skipped the class the majority of the prior semester. This semester I met someone that changed that…a white guy on the baseball team. He reminded me of Justin Timberlake. It was also the height of N'Sync's career. Our friendship was sort of instant. There was no sexual attraction just a connection. Our friendship even got me to come to class more and eventually him to start skipping class.

I would usually skip my 5th period class and not return to school

108

after lunch until dance practice. This semester was different. My new friend had an impact on me that was different than any other. I felt like I needed to get to know him as a person. I have had many of these meetings in life…people you meet and they play a part in changing you, or you them. Like winter or spring, they serve as a season in life that helps to shape you. As wild as I was sexually, I was still in church and open to change in my life.

We started to hang outside of class. The teen dance club scene was at its height. New teen nights were happening all over the city. My friends and I spent Thursday-Sunday nights in the teen clubs… dancing and partying…creating our mess together. What was really interesting about that season was that I was surrounded by so many other young men who were like me, broken and unaware.

Woody, my new friend, and I spent a lot of time talking…mostly on the phone at night. It was one of the most interesting times of my high school years. We talked about the day, his problems with his girlfriend and things that were going on in our lives. Our phone conversations became a ritual. A pouring out of sorts into each other. Some would say that it's here that soul-ties happen. I don't know about that, but a connection happened that was undeniable.
We were connected in a way I never experienced. Looking back I would describe myself as co-dependent. For the first time in a long time I had someone. I was exposed as a person to someone. I trusted Woody with my dreams and ideas. I cannot explain how this happened…I just know that I was open and honest for the first time. I think it was his innocence and genuine concern for me. It was the hope that someone was there for me and not the sex. Not even in my new friends had I found someone who was there for me and not my body.

There are some people you meet in life that allow you to be you… individuals who have found the freedom to be themselves and in return their presence gives you permission to let go of the mask you wear and just be. All that I wanted to be for others, he had become for me. He was a safe place to talk and dream. He did not see the dirt on me others had. The size of my penis had no bearing.

For the first time I had found someone who cared for me just 'cause I was me. Of course, those were not my thoughts at the time. For me, I was in love, as much as I thought I knew what love was. I loved to be around Woody. Our conversations at the end of the night would be my day's highlight. I could not function without the phone calls at night. There was joy in having someone care and to not have to sacrifice my body to do it.

I had no way of reconciling what I felt. Before meeting Woody, sex was a way of life. It had little to do with the person…it was more about the experience. It was them touching me and me them…them desiring me and wanting to have me. Most experiences would be without kissing, no intimacy and without a genuine connection. And after it was over I always felt unclean. I hated the person after the act for what I did to me. I served sex to be touched…to pretend I was loved and desired.

I never wanted those things from Woody. I wanted our friendship to remain pure. I cared too much for him to hate himself or me. I did not want him to feel the shame that comes after the encounter. He had no idea initially how I felt about him. I would hint to him but never say it for fear of losing my friend. Then my worse fear was realized. One day I pulled up at school with friends, late as always. When I got there I was met by a friend with news. He urgently grabbed me and said we have to talk. Woody had heard from a gossiping girl that I was into him.

My heart sank. I could hardly breathe. What choice did I have but to tell him the truth. However, I did not know exactly what the truth was. I knew I had no sexual desire for him. I was confused as to what I really wanted from our friendship. I loved Woody but not in a way that others could understand. I felt like I needed him to fill an emptiness I could not explain. I had no real explanation for how I felt. I had no idea how to explain a confused heart.

I went to class that day feeling like everyone knew about the situation. I feared they would all think I was gay…not because gay was bad but I thought having the title attached to me would ruin my future. I wondered what would happen when I became a preacher and got married. I thought of whether people would remember these events. Even in those times of confusion, I envisioned myself as a preacher with a family. It was settled I would be in ministry somewhere down the line. I wondered if it would ruin my chances at one day starting over. Would this be a stain I could not erase?

My friends and I skipped the next period that day, and Woody came with us. I knew I had to try to explain to him but had no idea how. After eating, we dropped my friends off and I drove him to the park near the school to talk. We sat at a park bench where and I fearfully told him I had to tell him something.
I stumbled through the words.

"So... I know you heard the rumor... it's true," I said.

I do not really know exactly what I had admitted to but I admitted to it dreadfully. I watched as his head fell into his hands and rose up to look at me completely red. His eyes were full of tears. I looked at him stunned by the reaction.
After a long a deep breath and long sigh he spoke. "I don't care… you're still my boy," he said.

I was relieved at his acceptance. We hugged, then I pushed him off me jokingly.

When we returned to school I told him to walk in before me so people would not see us together. I did not want to perpetuate the rumor. He refused…grabbing me and we walked in with his arm around me. Our friendship became stronger. He knew how I felt, although I could not understand it.

The acceptance became like a drug. He became my life and a reason to keep living. The few people who knew about how I felt were confused by how I acted. I never showed any feelings but now I could not help it. My closest friends who knew about my sexual exploits would ask what was happening with us. I insisted that I would never have sex with him. I did not want to hate him. I did not want him to know what it was to hate himself.

In this time my dad's family was busted for their involvement in drug dealing. It was devastating. Their involvement was grand, to say the least. At the end of it all, my aunt, three of my uncles, four of my great uncles, and a host of my cousins, both male and female, were all sent away to spend years in prison. The life of luxury I had grown so accustomed to ended.

I moved around from place to place. My best friend and I lived in my cousin's apartment in about 30 minutes outside of Nashville for a while. When the distance became too far, we finally settled in to his parent's home. They made me feel like a part of the family. I was going to school even less. I made up my mind to drop out but had not done it officially.

I shared with Woody a lot of my life and what I was going through. I confided in him, and he shared his dreams with me. Looking back on it we had a really unhealthy relationship. It was completely codependent. When we did not talk, I was depressed. I had given him power over me without knowing it. I was not in control of my emotions or thoughts. I was given to whatever would keep me in the place of acceptance and desire.

I felt the fact that he was someone who did not want to have sex with me in some ways freed me. It allowed me to feel something. I would wrestle with where our friendship was going to go. I knew I could not spend the rest of my life like this, but I would if he asked…only I could not have sex with him. I felt that if we had sex I would break him. I did not want him to carry what I carried. I wondered what

God would say about our friendship. I was conflicted in my heart but would do anything I could to stay in Woody's favor.

I became protective of him. No one could come too close without me having a say. I lost me in him. I did not understand what it was to love and be loved. Love was who loved you and would leave you…they died or moved away. The people who loved me showed me with sex. I did not know people who did not equate love by how far they could get with me sexually. What should have been a great friendship had become a deep connection that I could not explain or understand.

Our friendship went on for some time, then the inevitable happened. Woody met a new girl and fell in love with her. He began to push me to the side. When that happened it broke something in me. I had dropped out of high school by then. The rejection felt like it was too much for me. My world shattered. I spent days in the bed crying. I was no longer hiding my emotions. I was an obvious mess before all who knew me. My friend TJ skipped many days of school and spent some of her tuition money consoling me.

I cried over losing our friendship. I felt like I had no life without him. I had grown accustomed to abandoning everything for him. I had put all my energy into being accepted. The experience crushed me. It was a classic case of co-dependency. Now here I was… lost…a high school drop out with a broken heart.

I Am Shame

Memories flood my mind
Like time and feelings
Vivid and without apology
Bold and Accusing
Like Pain and Taste...Smell
I remember
I remember the exact moments
I let go. Wanting.
Desiring not able to control, Me
Passion in moments
Names not remembered
Giving all of me away
Nothing left to disgrace; I am sex.
Love or touch, feeling
Longing.
Look in my eyes...
Say my name... tell me you know my name
Do I make you feel good
Validate, Appreciate me
Am I Desired?
Wanted?
Kiss me.
Don't kiss me.
Lets get this over with
I remember
Nasty. Dirty. Pain.
I am Shame

Chapter Ten
Church Boy

I Am Redeemed

Present Like Light
Exposing me to me
Like Touch and Love
Intentional and with Grace
Gentle and Redeeming
Like peace and Smile...Kindness
I know
I know the exact moment
I gave in...Needing
Thirst not able to quench, Me
Healing in Moments
Remembered not Forgotten
Restoring who I am
Receiving all I'd lost, I am loved
Love and touched...Accepted
Filled. Acknowledged.
Whispers of destiny.
You know my name
You rejoice over me
You have validated, Appreciation
I am desired.
Wanted
Sealed
Forever I am sealed.
I am known
Beloved. Pure. Loved.
I am redeemed

During my high school years, the church I grew up in began to fall apart due to leadership. The pastor was eventually removed and the church closed. My mother's family had all grown up in the church. My older cousins had served as teachers and kept the church going. When the church was closed, it left a lot of us without a home church. My cousins and I would get together with our elder cousin Betty and pray that our church doors would be reopened. We missed the community that we had there. In the midst of all my family issues and the chaos of life, church was still a major part of life.

While I was living with my best friend, our prayers for our church were answered. We were sent a new pastor. He was sent from another church to pastor ours. They were a very intriguing couple. I had never seen a married couple act so lovingly. Their family reminded me of the Cosby Show. They modeled love in a way that I was not used to. They taught the Bible in a way that drew me in.

After being heartbroken by the Woody situation, I gave all of my time to the church. The church started a youth Bible study with the pastor's wife leading. I became her star pupil. The Bible became meat to me. I couldn't go a day without reading. I began longing for Sunday morning services. Wednesday night Bible Study was the week's highlight. The more I grew in my desire to study, the more I conflicted with my inner circle of friends still around me.

I began to see church in a completely different way than I used to. The thirst to be touched seem to subside. I was being challenged by what I was learning. I think, for my friends the noticeable change in me offended them. I started hanging less and less with them. After dropping out I was no longer with them at school. I would often sit silently in my room alone, praying and reading my Bible.

Woody was out of the picture and I had made the choice to pursue God, not fully knowing what that meant. There were times when my friends would walk in to find me laying prostrate on the floor praying and crying to God. They would find me lost in reading the

Bible. At times I was not aware that they were even around. They would walk around the room quietly looking perplexed at me. This went on for over a year. I didn't know what was going on with me. For the first time, I knew that there was something bigger than this hurt in me.

After some time the conflict of church life and friends was taking its toll. One Wednesday night after coming home from Bible study, I sat in the room alone...thinking. The house was filled with the family's visitors, but I was left alone thinking, "I can't keep doing this. I have to make a choice. I have to choose between the life of lasciviousness and the life that I am trying to pursue." My friends were not bad people...our lives were just heading in different directions. It was a painful choice I felt I had to make.

As I sat there on the bed, the tears begin falling. I cried silently to the Lord, "I choose you. I choose you." I told the Lord that if he would help me I would walk out of that house and serve Him. I called my aunt Mary that night and asked her to come and pick me up from my friend's house. I had no idea where I was going...no plan...no place to stay. I left the house trusting God to take care of me.

When she arrived to pick me up, I asked her if she would drop me at my paternal uncle's home. My grandmother was staying with him at the time. Due to the arrest on my dad's side of the family, they were living different lives than we were accustomed to. I left the house that night, and I did not look back. For the next few months I spent time on various couches...staying with people, not letting them know I was homeless.

My grandmother's sister had been arrested again and was sentenced to time in prison. Her arrest was on different charges than my other family members. While she was away, I stayed in her home with my cousin Vanessa. Every day was the same for me in that season of life. I would wake up in the morning, grab my Bible and read. I don't remember food or conversations with people.

The Bible was an ocean to me, and I wanted to drink it all in. When I was not reading, I was praying. The Word seemed to haunt me. It drew me in, and I wanted it all. I could not get enough of it. I had also seen something in these pastors who had come to my church that I wanted. They had shown me a God I never knew existed before. They had shown me wholeness that I had longed for. They became my father and mother. The church became my surrogate family.

Along with the new pastor came new church members. I spent most of my time at church. I lost myself in church, trying to find God. Whenever the doors were open, I was there. I believed I was meant for something great. I believed that my life had importance, but I had no idea what it was. I read countless stories of God using the least likely people, and it inspired me. The stories of God using a man that was an adulterer meant He could use me. I thought if he could use a murderer than I still qualified. I remembered the Preacher telling me I would be a preacher like him…the words I hated to hear him say. As a kid, I knew I would preach, although I was extremely shy in front of people. I promised myself I would not become like him.

I wrestled for months with my feelings and thoughts about ministry. There was a deep impression in me that God wanted me to use me. I felt God wanted to use my life and what I had experienced to help others. In this time I was often at the altar during invitation to discipleship crying. I wanted so badly to be used by God, but I had no idea how. I wrestled with whether or not to share the battle in my mind. My greatest fear was that I would become like The Preacher.

Finally I could not shake the impressions any longer. I went to the Pastor and told him God was calling me into the ministry. He smiled and said okay and gave me my first chore. He told me to cut my hair and start wearing a shirt and tie. My hair was still blonde from my high school days. I did as I was told. I could not afford dress pants so I wore my jeans with my shirts and ties.

The more I was in church the more it became me. My blonde hair was again its natural color. I got rid of my eyebrow piercing. Who I was before became a vague memory. That person had disappeared. He was never dealt with or addressed. He just stopped being. I moved on like high school never happened. I never talked about it, and no one ever asked. I moved forward with my baggage in-tow. It was hidden, but it was still with me.

I was hungry to be right before God. I gave all my time to service at church. I was a Minister-in-Training. I worked at the job more than I worked at my real job at a magazine shipping warehouse. The church flourished. I worked as one of the Youth Ministers helping oversee the youth department. I also sang in the choir and assisted in directing the choir.

The church acquired the building next door. It was a hair salon my entire life and was a fixture in the community. Purchasing the building was an unexpected miracle. The seller initially did not want to sell but we prayed for favor and got it. The building was purchased and paid off immediately. We called it "The Lazarus Building." It would aid in the church's vision of a ministry called "Project Lazarus." The ministry was to reach out to the community and those in need around us.

We gutted and cleaned the building. On Saturday mornings we begin working from the building. I would wake up at around 7am to hurriedly dress and open the doors of the Lazarus Building so we could start Saturday morning prayer meetings. These duties were normally the deacons' but most days it fell on me. We served the entire morning until the afternoon hours. In the early days we fed adults and talked with them. An organization came in to help start programming. We started a ministry for our neighborhood kids that I led. I began to work for the group that trained me to run the kids program.

I was young in ministry and having so much responsibility took its toll on me. I was not healed enough to handle it. However, I took the responsibilities seriously. I read the Bible every day without fail as often as I could. I wanted to pursue the truth of the Word. Sadly, I allowed no grace for myself or others in the pursuit. The way I presented myself was a man twice my age. My family members even began to change towards me.

My cousins with whom I went to church had called me by nickname all my whole life but now referred to me as Minister. Although they were all older than me, they respected me as a leader in the church. I was extremely hard on them, but not as hard as I was on myself. My sentences would often begin with "The Bible says" or "Pastor says." Seeking truth without grace was making me extremely religious.

I was a teacher's pet. I loved my pastors, and everyone knew it. I saw no flaws in the leadership in the beginning. This would bring some division in my family when they differed in their opinions of how the church should be run. I would always argue, "That's my Man of God" and I would defend him. Not since the death of my mother had I felt like I had a family unit. My pastors made me feel like I was their son.

Being so young I felt like I had something to prove to those who were older than me. I was the youngest person in leadership and youngest holding responsibility. I felt that I had to prove that my words had value. I sought to show that my call was just as valid. I lived the life I thought I was supposed to live with little compromise. We all have our ideas of what a minister was or a man called by God was… I tried to live that standard.

Even after I was twenty-one I did not drink alcohol. I would rebuke those who did, warning them to abstain from the very presence of what we had deemed evil. Once two of my cousins and our friend drank a wine cooler. When they made the plan to drink their wine coolers my cousin said to them, "We better not let Minister find out!" Eventually they ended up telling me, and I reprimanded them, as they knew I would. I was on the God squad, handing down my ideas of what was right and what was wrong. On the quest to live a life of accuracy in faith, I despised making mistakes.

It's ironic how our ideas of what righteousness and godliness are and how often we negate God's grace. For me to live and be accepted as a man of God…to present myself acceptable to the people…I was always told by leadership to dress a certain way. When I tried to grow my hair out I was made to cut it. I would walk into church when it had become about an inch and a half and be told "Cut your hair," almost nonchalantly.

I left the church and immediately headed to my uncle's to get a haircut. I thought I was submitting to authority, but I had succumbed to abuse of it. After this happened a number of times over the years I was told "The reason I tell you to get your haircut is because I wanted to make sure you were still submitting." I understood what he meant at the time. It made sense in the church's style of leading.

My family would treat me like an elder in the family. I was respected as a minister but felt like I was an outcast. The difference in treatment made me feel I was not a part of the family. It was like my title overtook my relationships with the people I had known all my life. I was no longer cousin, brother or nephew…I was The Minister. My title became my identity.

My aunt Mary was a Trustee at the church. She was a force to be reckoned with. She led with integrity and an iron fist. She was one of few that would speak out to leadership. She was never afraid to speak her mind. I admired her ability to serve and her fierceness. She served through her battle with cancer. Sometimes after treatments she could be found cleaning the church.

The church spilled into every area of life. If we were not at church together, then we were at each other's houses. We were excited to even spend Saturdays at the church without complaint. The choir began to grow as the congregation did. Sunday mornings were life-giving. I began to take courses and received my G.E.D. I applied for university and was accepted. The school was right down the street from the church and my community.

The university I chose was a Christian college. It was majority white with very few blacks. Another minister from the church also attended. Members of my family tried to convince me go to a cheaper university. I was determined to go to the one I had chosen. When I was accepted, I was elated.

 I quit my job at the warehouse and prepared for college life.
In my eagerness I failed to actually prepare financially. I was not aware that I needed to fill out a financial aid request. The day I went to move on campus I was surprised to find out that I needed to pay ahead of time. My college years would start with me not even having enough for tuition or housing. Luckily, the church took up an offering covering my tuition and allowing me to buy a book or two. I spent the first couple years without most of the books I needed.

 I moved into my cousin's apartment instead of campus. My cousin rarely even stayed home so I was alone most of the time. I was a full-time college student. I was broke with no car and now no job. Struggling to get back and forth to class proved difficult at times. I spent many days hungry and alone in the apartment. In that season hot-water cornbread became a meal. I was thankful for Sundays to hangout and eat with my church family.

My life became routine for the first time in years. I spent so much time at church and with church members I was often mistaken as the pastor's son. I looked up to him so much. He was known by his integrity. He and his wife were a great example to us all. He suffered from leukemia in the early years and still served, sometimes being carried into the pulpit. It was the integrity and the heart that the couple had for us that won over the community.

The pastor's wife was like light and love. I had never met a woman like her before nor since. She was regal. I don't think I've ever seen Jesus so embodied in one person as in her. She was a teacher by nature. She taught me so much in how she acted and interacted with those around her. There were countless times I would learn something new and share it with her. She would jump around and celebrate with me. She was just as excited as I was. Sometimes she already knew the lesson I shared but she celebrated that I got.

The two as a couple displayed love in a way that was infectious. There were nights where we would sit around their dining room table and he would teach me the Word. They were my first experience of what real loving relationship looked like in humanity. They modeled it within their family and with our church. We called her First Lady affectionately. Pastor was extremely strict. In the beginning I loved it…I felt I needed it. They were Mom and Dad to our close church family.

There was so much life and hope it bred family. I talked through things with my biological father around this time. One evening we sat on the phone for hours. I told him about what I was doing in ministry, and he was in tears. He began to apologize for not being there for me as a child. It was then I could actually look at the situation for what it had been. I considered the fact that he was just a kid when he had me. Although that doesn't excuse his behavior for me, it brought understanding. With that understanding came forgiveness. I wanted to allow him the role of father in my life. I was an adult but I welcomed the opportunity to be his son. Our relationship became better from then on.

Pharisee

The Pharisees have traded their robes
Daunting suits and ties calling themselves Sanctified
Woe to you, Pharisees!
Dressing up can't hide mess
Cleaning only the outside of the cup
Cloak or coat
You still have to undress to wash
To cleanse yourself
Pretenders we have become
Looking the part and lacking His heart
Seeking signs and wonders
While the lost wander
As the poor lay in hunger
Too consumed in our programs

Woe to you, Pharisee!
For we love the best seats in the house
We love to be greeted and celebrated in the public
Have we lost our way...
Cause I see him at Pool of Bethesda
Among those in need
While we sat in our comfy church seats
Trying to teach each other new ways to believe
Seeking new knowledge
And I hear him calling...
"My people are destroyed cause they don't Know me..."
They don't know me...Knowledge
No knowledge of me
Have we forgotten our way...

The Pharisees have traded their robes
Sporting heels and prayer clothes calling themselves Born Again
Laying hands and screaming tongues
Yet when the poor reaches his hand he is left empty

No words of comfort for the least
Cause we only see them at monthly outreaches

Have we stopped too soon
Have we reached the goal
Have we become the goal
We sit among ourselves judging ourselves
Making each other the goal
Seeking titles, praising position
Men have built for their king a throne
And pastors reign in his stead
Have we forgotten Him
Woe to you, Pharisees!
We lead men to become blind to truth
Teaching them to become like us..

The Pharisees have traded their robes
Clothed with Religion instead
Calling themselves Saved
Whoa...Cause I see him in me...
We who love well in church walls
Who cover up the fact that we fall
Have we forgotten that we are blood washed
Pharisee...
Serving so others will see
Forgetting the God in me
Covering myself with my own righteousness
Dressing up in my works
Whoa..
Pretender. Hypocrite. Actor
Feigning to have no issues
Woe to you Pharisees! The Pharisee in me..
The enemy to the God in me..

Chapter 11
Wounded Men

Wounded Men

Some of us carry wounds like fire on flesh melting
Blanketed with fear that suffocates you
I can't feel inside
I'm like Ice. Brick. Object.
Void of touch and sense
Wounds
Like broken glass cutting away at your insides
Sheltered with lies, shaming your integrity
I can give it, love
But don't know it
Wounds
Like poison killing you slowly
Covered with silence eating you from within
It's like I carry two men in me
One not living.
Inside, only comes alive when I dance
I carry him like weight...dead
Wounds
Like bleach on coloreds eating away at you
Not reachable but wanting to touch
To be Present and Here
To laugh or cry to perceive emotion
I'm stone within
Crumbling but not moving
Shaking but not shaken
Wounds
Like chasms in rock
Covered with leaves that only shade, no protection
Needing to cry to be heard, to love
To know what it is.
Wounded...Wounds
Like razors slicing away at your veins
Bandaged with shame, silence and lies
Some of us are Wounded Men

As time passed, I grew and changed…so did my ideas. I spent many years submitting to church authority without thought. I was losing myself in the process. My dreams became whatever the church dream was. My vision was attached to whatever the mandate for church was. I did not know who I had become. I think from the time I turned eighteen until I was twenty-three I only missed about three services. The ones I missed were due to being out of town for work with the organization I worked for.

I donned suits, ties and low haircuts…presented the demeanor of a man well seasoned in years. I did what I thought was expected of me. I was having a rough time one Sunday. It must have been evident on in my face. One of the older ministers reprimanded me. "Why do you look so down? Change your countenance. You can never let the people see your countenance down," I was told.

Under the pressure of being a leader, I was breaking. I struggled with the desire to have sex again. The longings seemed to be peaking in my stress. I was committed to not giving in. Although I felt I could not tell anyone what I was dealing with I was determined not to fail. The battle went from my mind to watching porn. I struggled secretly.

I wore my mask without realizing it…I put it on with the suits and ties. I used it to cover up the hurt I was not allowed to share. Dressing up for Sunday service no longer only meant clothing myself. I began pretending like nothing else was going on outside of what I was doing. The joy of the Lord had not become my strength but a phrase I used to shield my plight. I had a false joy I carried on Sunday mornings. It covered inner turmoil.

Sometimes we build exteriors that become cells, and we live in those cells like prisoners…hoping someday something will happen to set us free. I had grown accustomed to being the minister so many people looked up to that I believed my lie. I was the guy who had mastered presenting the perfect countenance, yet on the inside I was

130

struggling secretly with a past that I could not share. I wrestled with hurts that I could not reveal…longing began to overwhelm me. The life that I had forgotten I once lived was calling me. The man I thought was dead I still carried in me.

Once for a class I had to write an essay sharing my testimony of meeting Jesus. In sharing my testimony I talked a little about my sexual encounters as a child. I made the mistake of sharing my paper with a leader in the church. After reading it he said asked if I really had to share so much. He advised to share a cleaner version. In a culture steeped in religion and tradition, it was important to be seen in a certain way. A minister was to walk before the people near blameless…presenting themselves as ones who have attained a certain standard of righteousness. You do not have struggles… you have opportunities to overcome. There is no weakness just "The Devil" trying to kill your minister. You feign wholeness…covering brokenness with a faith disposition. You suffer silently so the people you lead can be encouraged by your right way of living. The church culture I was in was keeping me captive to it.

Others had come from a church far stricter than mine had become. People would tell us stories of ministers having to sign in when they arrived to church. This culture of giving our lives to the ones who led us had become slave-like in its mentality. Having to ask permission to leave town or give reason why you would not be at church on a particular Sunday served to imprison. There was no freedom.

I loved my leaders and I always knew that their intentions in leadership came from a sincere place. My leadership and I grew to have a love-hate relationship. I was becoming a rebellious son questioning authority. They were my family, and I loved them… but being in such a close relationship with them and so close to my church family, I felt trapped.

I had become the picture of the minister we all know. But behind that picture lay a canvas of a man still not sure of who he was. The idea of what a man really looked like in that world was painted with every masculine stereotype you could imagine. The men of the church carried the same persona. They were family men, and in the midst of them I was a pretender.

I was not pretending that I was any less of a man, but that I was just as unbroken as they were pretending to be. We all wore our suits on Sunday mornings. We laid hands, praying and ministering… pretending… like underneath it we were complete and whole. Male or female, we all stood before the people as examples…not broken… not vulnerable and far from transparent…pretending.

There were many days while teaching that I would share glimpses of my past experiences but it was always met with looks of taboo. I was a prisoner in the jail that I had help build. I don't blame my leadership or the church… it was all we knew to do. The culture of religion and false sense of upright living had wiped out all that was grace…we feared brokenness.

Throughout the years the climate of tradition had robbed us of our own lives and of our freedom. It took from us the ability to be individuals in the midst of community, and so we all pretended. Yearning to become like our pastor or to be the next Bishop T. D. Jakes, Juanita Bynum, or whoever was at the height of religious Christendom at the time.

I don't think we knew what was going on. We were lost in an uphill battle, trying to become what we preached Christ had already made us. It was a conflicting reality of suits, ties and performances… living but not knowing who I was. I was struggling to come to grips with my childhood and its confusion. I was captive to myself… in bondage to what I had been and who I had become. This truth without grace had led me to religion. And religion had become a thief robbing me of life. I wanted something different but did not know what that was or how to get it.

The church would have visiting churches in often. We would visit other churches as well. It was customary for churches to fellowship, sharing a meal and a service together. During one of the fellowships I met a guy who was also in ministry. He was more than ten years older than me. He was a good-looking guy and very muscular. He dressed very clean in his suit and tie. He had a polished look. He caught all the ladies' attention when he walked into the room.

On this occasion while our churches were sharing a service, he introduced himself and gave me his number telling me we should keep in touch. We hugged as brothers do in the church...shaking with one hand and embracing with the other. In the embrace, he seemed to flex all his muscles. I knew then what his motives were. Months passed but to my surprise one evening he reached out to me. We spent an evening talking on the phone.

During the call he wanted to let me know he was not like the other ministers and that he had a life outside the church. I was not used to a minister who spoke like he did. As the conversation progressed he was sharing stories of strippers and parties he had been too. It was intriguing to me. I did not have friends that spoke like he did.

Outside of preaching abstinence, sex had been a taboo subject for me. As we talked the old me seemed to awaken. I was wrapped up in his stories and the flirtatious conversation. He asked me my sex history and I gave enough to allow him to know I was not innocent. It was almost a relief to share some of what I had done. Only with him it was not a testimony... it was a pattern for him to weave into.

He became my escape from the religious monotony. The longings could no longer be suppressed through porn. We began a sexual relationship shortly there after. He was far more affluent, and so he provided the places to meet. When we were together, he spoiled me. He claimed he had never had sex with a man, yet his pursuit and cunning ways said otherwise. He introduced me to "poppers." I did not know what they were at the time. They are used to heighten the sexual experience typically used in homosexual sex.

During these times I was full of guilt and shame. We saw each other occasionally when it was convenient. Eventually we moved on from each other. I did not see anyone else for a while. I was overwhelmed with guilt. The longings that aroused again did not leave. The demon I had awakened had again taken me… this time stronger than before. I would spend countless hours on the internet or phone chat-lines with strangers.

The urges for sex and body contact grew stronger. On an AOL chat I met a guy I chatted with for a while. As we chatted he told me he wanted to meet. I was afraid at first to meet a stranger in person. I told him I could not risk being found out. He told me he was in a similar situation. He eventually told me that he was one of the pastors at a large church.

I agreed to meet him but told him we could only talk. We agreed that we would only meet and talk over dinner. We pledged not to have sex. It was at this dinner that I had my first taste of alcohol since I was eighteen. After dinner we had sex for the first time. He and I began a secret sexual relationship. After each encounter the shame would again take me.

I was losing myself in sex again. It began to control me. It became all I thought about. I did not have control of myself…it moved it. The chat-line and internet chats became sexual hook ups with strangers. It had me, and I could not control myself. I led two lives… the minister that people saw on Sunday and the addict I became when I was alone.

The pastor I met online and I became close. He would visit me nearly daily while I was in university. He would drop by and bring me lunch. I was thankful being a struggling student. We at one point tried to blend our secret life in with our outward lives as ministers. It was a short-lived effort.

One evening he brought me to his church to show me around. After showing me around we ended our trip in the church offices. In the office I met the main Assistant Pastor and then one of the janitors who was cleaning. She greeted me and the Assistant Pastor and then my counterpart. As we were walking out the door, she asked him how his wife was doing with the pregnancy.

The question startled us both. His face tried to hide the fact he knew he was exposed. He answered her as we walked out. I do not know what he said…I was shocked to find out he was married. When we got to the car we sat quietly. I finally vented my disappointment and frustration. Not only was I sleeping around with someone… the person was married.

We moved on from that anger and after a few weeks continued our secret life. I did not feel for him as a person. When he was not around I did not think of him or miss him. While he was there he served to fill longings in me. When he was not around I also met up with others from the internet or chat-line. Most of my partners were white, straight or bi couples. I was active with male and female. I preferred white since it was easier to keep it a secret. Sex was my master, and I served it.

My life at church continued, although not as normal. I was a mess with what I was hiding and the constraint I felt in ministry. I knew something had to change. One Saturday I spoke at church and talked briefly about being molested as a child. It was a cry for help. After I spoke I was not met with any conversation or opportunity to talk, only compliments on a good message. My grandmother had come to hear that sermon. It was a rare thing for her to come to church.

As I changed and grew so did my leadership at church. We could not see eye to eye on many things. I was no longer as apt to submit to the same type of strict authority. I started to visit some of my friends' churches and saw how different they were. I was searching for anything different to get me out of the mess I created.

I needed to silence the longing again.

Some wounds you expose to be healed others you leave covered treating them until they are healed. My childhood wounds were covered but not treated. They lay in me like a cancer spreading becoming evident to me in every sexual encounter. I became numb to the acts of sex then. It was just a way of life. It was the means to cope. All those years there, and I had not shared my struggle with anyone. It was becoming too much.

I wrestled with leaving the church. I knew a change had to be made but did not know how. I talked to the leadership about the restlessness, feeling stuck at the church. To my surprise, very little care was shown. I was told that sometimes when building big machines come in and do the hard work and then they move on. They move on so someone else can come along. The words hit me like a ton of bricks. The very leaders to whom I had given my life hurt me.

Slave

Smell like liquor
Mixed with sweat and funk
Taste like dirt
Feels like shame
I cant stop
Sniff
Poppers
Pushing me through
I just need to be touched
Told I am special
Desired
Willing to risk it all
Slave

Chapter Twelve
Coming Home

This Is Love

He calls in whisper
Reminding of times past
Memories like love
Overtaking mind and body
Softly He's speaking
Tone pulling you
Voice drawing you in
This is what love sounds like
He speaks only what you two know
Reminding you of secret times
Whispering your heart
Recounting His heart for you
Calling you closer
Make you yearn for all He is
This is what love feels like
He touches places only He can
Speaking so gently
Tears rolling down cheek
Smile paints face
You deep sigh this love
Amongst room's noise
He is all that is heard
He has become all that exist
This is what love is
He calls you back to Him
Back to places forgotten
Whispering His love
You sigh its Peace
Feel Him in You like life
This is Love

The Sunday after my conversation with the leadership, I attended church with a friend. It was an Episcopalian church. The sermon that Sunday was about the sacrifice of a son, Abraham and Isaac. The priest spoke of giving up something you love for God. That day the church I had grown up in became the son I had to give up. It had been my love for so many years and it was time to walk away if only for a season, and I did.

I spent about six months at the Episcopal church. It became sort of a sabbatical for me. The church was predominately white. The services were completely different that what I was used to. I welcomed the change. I joined the College Ministry. I continued my work with the organization that helped start our kids' ministry. I had become a regular employee. I began living with the organization's leaders…a couple I had grown close to over the years.

I moved in after we came home from doing ministry in a Florida camp. The camp was located in Northern Florida. It was on trips to this camp that a sense of freedom was awakened in me. My first trip there I spent one week and then was asked to come back and counsel and volunteer the final two weeks. I was excited to take on the adventure.

During camp, I came alive. The time with the kids was so precious. Every week there allowed me the freedom to be away from all my demons. There I was not a minister or an addict. I was free… if only for those few weeks.

While living with the family I learned a lot about myself and religion. It was during those times that I found out white people have the Holy Ghost too. The wife and I performed together in the organization. She was a woman of staunch faith and integrity, and so was her husband.

At work we became close and gelled well. I took on more responsibility for the organization and it became a part of me. I noticed that the messages we were teaching were impacting my life. The message of Hope and Character began to mold my relationships.

At the house, our organization's message of "Getting Along" was put to the test. It was a gigantic five bedroom home, situated in the heart of downtown Nashville. Also living in the house was the couple's son, baby daughter, and Lauren, a female friend who also worked for the organization. They were very gracious people. I learned much from the couple about business and leadership. Things were not always happy, but I felt welcomed.

The husband and I spent much time together talking and working with the organization. His heart was truly to see people changed and to help the least among us. Eventually he began the process of becoming a priest during this time. We started a house church called My Father's House, which flourished. My demons subsided in this season. I was too busy to think about anything other than church.

In this time my circle of friends began to broaden. I became close to two guys from the Episcopal church and spent most of my weekends with them. I also became close friends with my female roommate and her friends. There was a guy named Akil that joined us at house church, and we became close friends. He was the only other black guy. There were not many in the circles I hung in.

Akil went to a church outside of Nashville that he kept telling me I needed to check out. I was attending the Episcopal church for 10:30am service…later the Pentecostal church for their afternoon service…then ending the night at My Father's House. I was trying to meet all my spiritual desires…trying my best to stay in the right frame of mind.

Sometimes church serves as a hiding place. The place you go to escape your demons. You run to it and hide deeper in it, trying to cover what plagues you. What we fail to realize in running is, we cannot outrun ourselves. Services had become my beard, hiding my face from myself. I needed church to keep me from myself.

I began to attend a College Ministry with Akil called Worship Culture. My Father's House fizzled out and I moved into my own place up the street from the couple. Worship Culture became the place I needed to fill the need for community. I was missing my home church. Worship Culture met on Monday nights.

There was a large group of us, mostly Belmont University students. Monday night was a ritual I dared not miss. It reminded me of the old days of church. We would spend hours in worship and prayer for each other. We would prophesy and love on each other. Guest speakers would come in from all over to share with us. Some of the most prominent leaders in the prophetic and evangelical movements of the church would come speak at our meetings.

It was in this time that I added my old church's 8am service to my Sunday morning rituals of services. I was often met with reasons why I should come back. I was not interested in returning initially. One particular Sunday that changed. I went into my home church for 8am and headed to the Episcopal church for the 10:30am service.

When I got to the doors I felt I heard, "Go Home." I paused in the vestibule and took a deep breath. I stood for a second knowing what that meant for me. I then turned went back to my car and went to my home church. I was met with surprise and excitement from the members. The sermon at the eleven o'clock was fitting. It was about Abraham sacrificing Isaac. The same sermon the Episcopal priest had given six months earlier. The difference in the message was his emphasis. He preached, God always gives you back the thing you love. I came back home that Sunday.

I resumed most of my positions in the church. I went to choir rehearsal the next Saturday. Normally you have to attend three rehearsals to sing, but I was allowed to sing after just one rehearsal. I directed the choir again that same Sunday. I was home, and for a while it was different. I was also different due to what I had experienced in the other churches. I had gained my own way of looking at things and was no longer the young kid in ministry. I had become a man in those six months away.

After that Sunday I talked with the leadership about my ideas for the choir and the ministry. I had left a slave to the house, but I returned a son. I learned much about leading worship and being led by the Spirit from my time at camp, Worship Culture and the other churches I visited. I was given the opportunity to use what I learned.

I became the church's first Worship Leader. I was now a paid employee of the church. I only made twenty-five dollars initially but it meant a lot to me in those days. The choir and the ministry became my life again. I was a strict leader…still truth with little grace.

This was a season of refreshing for me. When I came home this time it was like revival swept the church. I think it was the mind set we were all in. The musician leading before I returned caused tension in the choir, but when I came home we were rejuvenated. God was doing something with us all. I created a praise team. The pastor's son, the pianist, and I began experimenting with the music.

The church continued to grow. I took on more responsibility. I was not ordained or licensed yet, but I had more responsibility than most of the others who were. Our small building became packed out every Sunday. Most services were standing room only. People came to hear the message or just to hear the choir sing.

I led with vigor, sometimes almost more dancing and celebrating than leading. People would come because they saw that we were hungry. We would worship out of our desperation for God. I was more myself leading worship than anywhere else. I was broken in worship. I could be a complete mess before people…hands lifted singing songs with tears flowing. Most worshiped God 'cause He was so good. My tears most days were brokenness and shame desiring deliverance from demons I knew I still hid.

My urges for sex were less frequent but still there. There were moments of break down where sex would call and I would go without thought or protest. Nights where I would drive to have sex, tears rolling down my face. Those times when I did not want to go but felt I had no choice...sex controlled me. When it called, I answered...most of the time not even knowing my partner's real name.

I continued going to Worship Culture and participating with them. On Friday Nights I began going to the church Akil told me about outside of Nashville. My first night there was amazing. That night was a teaching on the Prophetic. During the service they wanted to practice the prophetic and needed a volunteer. Instead of getting a volunteer, they chose me.

The idea was for the volunteer to stand up and for people to come up and receive prophetic words from the congregants. I still have the words from that night... words that encouraged me and served to keep me in the season. I then took on a new routine instead of my Sunday Morning ritual of churches. Monday Night was Worship Culture... Wednesday I taught at church...Friday was Akil's church... and the weekend I was at my home church.

First Lady

She came like sun
Wrapping around you expelling the night
Love led her
Spirit moved her
Mother to all
She was a lady
Friend and Hope
I like heir followed
She lead me to light
She was regal
Like time, Ageless
Grace and Teacher
She shined and we glowed in her light
I like child learned from her
She taught me love
Faith and Celebration
Strength to all
She encouraged me
Made me believe
Preacher and Wife
She was like Him
And I like son loved her

Chapter Thirteen
My Travels

Pain

Scars
Can they heal?
Pain that I feel, will it ever go away?
So much pain.
Help me, help me bear. This Pain.

I again sit with those who are stronger than they know
They are strength and power
Wisdom beyond their years
Can I wish it away?
Can you take it away?
Can I erase what they have seen?
Pain
They carry and shed no tears
And they trust in God in ways only they can explain
Raped by their fathers
Losing their mother
Suffering from disease
Jesus, I cry, Help them please...
Pain
Take it away
Wash it away
Will they ever know life without it?
It's too hard for me to see
Lord, take it away
Their pain

Scars...
Can they heal?
Pain that I feel
Will it ever go away?
So much pain
Help me, help me bare it

I took my first trip outside of the country to São Paulo, Brazil. It was there I experienced 3rd world poverty for the first time. Driving through the rainy city I saw a man wrapped in a trash bag trying to keep warm. A way of living that seemed foreign to me. The poverty and lack displayed in the city troubled me.

In the eyes of poor Brazilian kids I saw Jesus. For the first time I touched the God that I knew to be real through their hugs and handshakes. The trip impacted me heavily. It provoked me to dream of doing something greater than I was. It was then that, "the call" I had so honestly expressed earlier in my life had meaning outside of what I had given myself to.

While in Brazil I experienced some miraculous things. I spent my whole life hearing about a God that healed. For the first time I encountered healing. In a service a woman's tumor disappeared…a thought that would seem unbelievable to any skeptic. I would not have believed it had I not witnessed it myself. The miracles went on and on. From kids walking out of their wheelchairs for the first time to people who were deaf gaining the ability to hear. Legs grew out to be even. My mind was being blown by the miracles.

The encounter that had the most impact was with a street kid. We had seen many diverse miracles and things happening on this trip. However, this encounter sticks with me as vivid as this morning's sun. Our team had been given a day off. We were outside walking through a park when we entered a Catholic church. It was a dark place. There were people in the pews. We looked around some of the relics, observing the rituals of the monks. Eventually, we left to see more of the park.

While walking around we decided that we would pray for people. Outside the church we met two little kids. The older one was about fourteen and the younger no more than ten. They were brothers. The younger of the two walked on crutches. His leg was deformed…one leg shorter than the other. It was not unlike others we had seen grow even in our meetings. I remember looking at this kid and feeling so sad for him. Our group gathered around the kid to pray for him.

As our translator spoke to him in Portuguese, we all prayed. I remember laying my hands on his shoulder and feeling jolted on the inside. Pictures of his home, family and his life flooded my thoughts. I could hear his small voice inside of me. I could literally hear his prayers in my thoughts.

We spent a little while praying for him and those prayers haunted me the entire time. I asked questions while we were praying to confirm the images that were flashing through my head. He confirmed they were all his reality. At prayer's end we walked away and left him there. He was not healed. I don't even know if he was affected by this session, but I was.

As we walked away, I tried to hide my tears. I kept looking back to see where he was going. I needed to know he was going to be okay. I cried uncontrollably trying to stay distant from my team. This experience had wrecked my heart. This was the first time that I had experienced what we deem the least of these and I did not know how to help him.

We got back to the hotel that night and I tried to journal about the experiences of the trip. I wanted to share what I had learned throughout our time there. I was trying to conclude my couple of weeks of journals with how blessed the trip had been. Yet, the only memory that I could hold on to was touching this little boy. Something inside of me whispered, "This is what you are to carry back."

My heart had broken by what I encountered. Those who have been rendered voiceless stayed on my mind. I was impacted by the fact that prayer alone cannot always help. The church life I had lived before this trip became a conflict within. When I returned home from my trip to Brazil I looked at our church and our community with different eyes. I wasn't satisfied with the gospel we had become so accustomed to in America. There was something greater. There was a cause greater than ourselves.

The saying "In losing your life you'll find it" now had meaning to me. I wanted to find life in giving myself up for those who did not have. I was intent on using my voice to speak for those who otherwise would not be heard. It became harder and harder for me not to speak up against our tradition and religious acts. I wanted to speak for the poor and oppressed…to speak for the broken boys. My style of preaching and teaching changed.

My first sermon after Brazil echoed my contempt.

"We need to die, die to ourselves," I proclaimed.

I was frustrated with our way of ministering.

I asked throughout the sermon, "What are we doing?! What…are… we…doing?!"

I was no longer satisfied with church as usual. I was inside the church, hungry for freedom while people starved on the outside. I was thirsty for solutions.

After my trip I came back excited to change our community and church. I was met with heartbreak. First Lady who had struggled with sickness for sometime had become very ill. I went to visit her for what would be my last time. She was as sweet as ever. She greeted me with the biggest smile.

"Hi, son," she said as I made my way upstairs to see her.

My cousin Deana and I had come to spend time with her. Deana was near tears when she saw her.

First Lady said, "Don't start that crying." She smiled and we spent the next hour talking and catching up. Not many days after she went to Jesus.

We handled the death of her like a bad business deal at church. We were told not to cry or show our hurt. The day I found out she was not getting well, I was told before I walked on stage to lead worship. I was called to a quick meeting. I was told she was dying soon so we need to be prepared. I was to lead worship and not let the congregation know what was going on.

I went to the back of the church and broke down crying. I tried to hide my emotion but was joined by two other leaders. We consoled each other, hiding our pain from those we led. I was losing my mother again and had to be strong yet again. I went out to the stage and lead worship like nothing was happening. I lead like I knew no hurt...smiles on faces like paint, clownish how we pretend.

Leadership did not take a break after her death. No one was afforded the opportunity. We continued on with the mission. We gave ourselves to building the ministry and a new building. If we hurt we covered it with ministry and secret tears.

Brazil had shifted my heart. I was on a mission to see the world. Suddenly, the word that God had spoken to my heart all those years ago meant more than just church work. The call to serve became a bigger thing to me than just helping out at out local meetings. My heart was shifting, and I was so conflicted with where I was yet again.

I met a couple at a local coffeehouse who were enrolled at a Missions school in Antioch. We talked a little about what they were doing and about the school. I was sold almost immediately at the chance to learn more about missions. A few months later I moved out of my apartment and went to Missions school to prepare for my move to a foreign country. I moved in with six other guys into an apartment in

Antioch. I shared a room with two of them. They were all younger than me. I was the only African-American in the entire school. The school was only about 60-70 people including staff. It was an interesting season.

The school was not what I had envisioned it to be. However, it challenged everything I had believed about church and religion. It shattered some of what I thought were foundational teachings. The Devil had less power than I once believed…turns out Jesus rose with all power. Satan was no longer God's nemesis. I began to learn the difference between the Spirit and law. Grace began to mix with truth. Their language of community and servanthood hit home.

It was like they were able to put words to what my heart had been feeling. Though I learned a lot from the school it was not a good fit for me. The life that the community was moving toward was not a life I wanted. It had become another form of the religious chain grasping me. I disagreed with some of the community's way of life. The place challenged and discouraged me. I stayed for one year and left…my demons still accompanying.

I moved in with my aunt Cherry for a while before I got my own place. By then she was no longer drinking like she had in previous years. She moved into her own house outside of the community I had grown up in. Her son Kevin was the only person still living at home. Kevin was the mentally challenged cousin who had in our early years thrown the puppy. He now refused to be called Bunch and would only answer to Kevin.

I began building new relationships with my family. I was no longer as stern as in years past. I was still Minister but more introspective. My secrets were too many to stand in judgment of anyone else. Most of our family had moved from the projects and were scattered throughout Nashville.

My aunt Mary had died from breast cancer a few years earlier. My sisters were both living their lives. We all seemed to have escaped the horror of the hood. It all seemed to be a distant memory. I thought the fearful nights of gunshots were all gone. My new sense of peace was soon shattered. One night while sleeping on the couch I was awaken by a loud crash. I opened my eyes to find two men pointing guns in the doorway. One of them had an AK-47 pointed directly at me. The other held a smaller handgun scanning the room. He yelled for me to get down on the ground. Awakened so suddenly, I was still drowsy. I slid from the couch to the floor.

As I sat on the floor trying to make out the faces of the men in the dark, I prayed. I was afraid... seeing the gun pointed directly at me. My life was flashing before my eyes. I tried to remind myself of things I still wanted to do in life. I tried to reconcile that it could all be over in this moment.

Suddenly my cousin Kevin opened the door of his room. His room was situated next to where the men were sitting. One of the guys screamed for him to get down. I sat watching...stunned. Kevin took off running down the hallway. The guy with the handgun fired at him. I knew in that moment my life was about to end.

After the flash of light from the gunfire the room went dark again. The men had taken off running the opposite way of my cousin. The bullet barely missed Kevin as he ran through the doorway and out of the back of the house. We all survived the bandits. For many nights, I could not sleep. The hood life of my childhood had again shown its face. I moved out very soon after that.

Poet's Prayer

May my words paint pictures
Give hope. Transition. Be a light
Cause some people can't see the way out
Let me be a light to the world
Some Salt to this earth
And let my words Paint Pictures
Give hope. Transition
Some have lost their way
And emptiness holds them too close
Death. Dying. Lost.
Missing something
Needy.
May my words Paint Pictures
Give hope. Transition. Be a light.

154

Chapter Fourteen
Stepping Into The Darkness

Gulu Boys

I have sat with giants, who stood smaller than me
And they tell me stories
Of what seems like ancient times
Of Battles and survivals that hold horror my poetry would fail to
convey
I sat with giants and listen to their stories and stared into their
eyes
These eyes tell me more stories than they know
Though some don't speak at all they tell me stories
They teach me
I dare not speak because word... my words fail me
So I sit and I stare
I learn from giants

He speaks...
He stands 5'8 and a half and all I can see from where I sat are his
eyes
He was a solider before puberty and his eyes tell it all...They are
unreal
How can a giant so young have eyes that outnumber both he and I
combined in years
And when he speaks my eyes are open and I see him
No longer invisible
I see him and his words haunt me...
"I was a good solider, I was a real good solider," He whispers
And those words vibrate through and through me
He sits there, eyes filled with tears that dare not fall
He half smiles and half chuckles
Not knowing whether to be sad or proud of his achievements
A conflicting reality I will never understand
No one even flinches at these words that I cannot comprehend
They all sit and stare into worlds I have never seen

Memories flooding them that they try and forget
I look at them and wonder where they are
This place they travel is deeper than I know
A deep that was has been dug by pain and suffering I cannot wrap
my mind around
Yet everything in me longs to go to where they are and heal them
These who sit in front of me
Though they are just boys
They are giants that my heart yearns to hold and console
To erase their fears and pain
They are giants
They tell me stories
They teach me

Encountering truth that partnered with grace shook me at my core. I was no longer comfortable with the lies I led. I longed for the grace to be open and vulnerable. I yearned to be real and open in my brokenness. The desire became apparent to those closest to me.

We built our new church building a couple of years after First Lady died. When we finally walked into that building, we were different. The church was no longer the small church on the corner with a Project Lazarus building. That building was gone, and so was its vision. We had changed, the mission had changed and my mask was changing.

We had become a self-sufficient church. We were no longer under our mother church in downtown Nashville. We were no longer a family like previous years. The time we spent at church became more chore than celebration. Leaders became more like employees than clergymen. Though no one was paid, we operated more as business counterparts than a family.

We lost who we had been in the little building. The building was beautiful, but behind the brilliant painting of harmony and love was dissonance and resentment. I was trapped in our religious duties. I had lost myself in my leaderships' dream. The building and our appearance took precedence. I was given to leaders who led me only by what they were told. In the beginning, I followed blindly. This was my home and I loved it, but too much of me was tied up in the chains I bore.

I was frustrated with so much…but mostly with myself. I was longing to be free of the longings and to break free of the slavery religion had me in. I wanted freedom from the bondage of my sexual addiction. I was tired of wearing my mask. I needed reality. The life I was living was killing me. I battled with depression. To escape sex I turned to the church…to escape religion I turned to sex.

Addiction can happen without one even knowing it. All the years I was serving sex and did not see it as an addiction. It called my name, and I answered. I hated myself and did not know it. I was giving myself away for just a touch. There were times when I had sex, and I would not climax. I would have sex with partners and allow them to climax but would not myself. A part of me hated the climax. With the climax came the guilt. It was then that I felt dirty and unclean.

My sexual partners were not people I knew...they were nameless strangers. I would go by some alias...make up some story of why I was in town or why I had to be discreet. Some were male identifying as gay, bisexual or even straight. There were also couples, male and female, who enjoyed the company of black men. They were people that desired my body and would keep my secret.

Initially, after the encounters I would shower for long periods of time...crying and praying as the water ran over me...scrubbing myself...trying to wipe away the memory...praying Psalm 51... hoping that the soap and water would purge me of the shame. Eventually I became numb. I would commit the acts and leave. After I left it was like it never happened. I would not even acknowledge it within myself.

Then there were nights that I left a service full of hope. Then sex would call me late in the morning hours when I was alone. I would awake it and fulfill its desires without feeling for myself or others. I was growing tired of being numb. I wanted to feel again. I wanted people to be human...heart again and not just flesh. I wanted to feel clean. I bore the lies and hid behind them. I was crumbling behind my mask...covering sexual addiction with religion.

Maya Angelou was once quoted as saying, "There is no greater agony than bearing an untold story inside of you." I was carrying that agony, and it spilled over into everything I was doing. I was hurting and near killing myself with sex and no one knew it. The lie was crushing me inside. I noticed that I had very little tolerance for anything that was not the truth. I hated my lie. I loathed me. I found myself becoming more and more vocal in my disdain for religious monotony.

The thought to just tell people the truth seemed simple, but as a leader in the church it was not. It's hard when the truth opposes the systems we have set up. I became a rebel in the church. My frustration, my hurt and my secret struggles stewed together resulting in anger. I was angry at the lack of concern for the community, lack of brokenness one to another and at myself for living my lie. I was still pretending…wearing my suit and tie like leaves covering my nakedness…broken yet quiet, living yet dying…realizing I couldn't maintain my silence.

The burden I was carrying was heavy on me. I wanted to know what it was like to know who I really was. I needed to know the truth behind the mask I wore. I was a slave to my secret. I was enslaved to my untold story. The only difference now was I wanted to be free. For me, freedom was an all-inclusive word. I wanted to tell my story. I wanted the freedom to be broken and not keep pretending like I had all of my stuff together. I wanted to care about somebody other than myself or my church. I wanted all the things I lost along the way. I wanted to love and feel loved. I wanted to not have to be strong for my sisters or the congregants.

I questioned what to do when all you know has become something you loathe…when all you thought was truth seemed to hold lies. Church politics seemed no different from the politics of the world. The masks I wore were slowly falling away.

I dreamed of a place of brokenness and grace. Living in anything other than that truth tormented me. I had an idea of what it was to love…to put someone before yourself and to lay down your life for your brother, yet what church had become was completely opposite…not just my church…it was all over. Everywhere I went I saw the same sickness.

We had turned what was supposed to be a living, thriving body into a business. Our goal wasn't to see people free and alive but rather to see the business flourish. Many of us had given our life to the business and in doing so we neglected true ministry. In that we had lost ourselves.

The desire for freedom was all I could think about. My church held a big place in my heart…still does today. Every trip I took and every encounter that I made I thought of how it could benefit them. I loved the kids like they were mine. However, I realized I needed to get better for me. I needed to stop leading to follow.

I resigned from all of my leadership roles in church. It was a Sunday morning when I had the peace to step down. The gospel choir was singing, giving me a day off. I did not have many opportunities to sleep in so I slept in through 8am service and was going to visit another church for their 11am service. We were visiting another church that evening, so I planned to be there to lead the choir.

That morning I was awakened by phone calls from the leadership. I didn't answer the calls but was left voice messages. I called back instead of checking them. The leadership was irate with me about missing 8am service…blaming me for the lack of youth attendance. I was accused of only doing what I do for the money. I was paid $100 a week as a worship leader. In a church our size, normal worship leaders hold salary positions that paid at least $25,000/year.

When I stepped down, I was the Youth Minister, Worship Leader, a Choir Director and served in other ministries. I helped with the kitchen staff, oversaw kid outreach leadership and taught the dance team. I was at church at least 3 days a week. I was amused at the accusation of being there for the money. I apologized for my absence and said I would be there for the 3pm service.

I was asked why I would be at another church if I could not come to my own. I was told if I did not come to the 11am service then I

162

should not pretend at the 3pm service. The conversation was not loud, but the anger from the other end was evident. Throughout the conversation I remained calm. We ended the conversation…them stewing and me at peace.

When I hung up the phone it was like the peace washed over me. I whispered to myself that it was time. I went to the 3pm service as I planned but not expecting to lead. I had received calls from the choir telling me the leadership planned on calling me out if I got up to lead. I was not angry and harbored no ill feelings. To me it meant it was simply just time to move forward.

Of course, my resignation was not received well. It resulted in a bit of confusion for the laypeople.   I was ostracized by some of the leadership. But when you have experienced grace in truth and know it to be real, you cannot escape it…it is hard to live a lie. My resignation had nothing to do with anyone else. It was about me moving into a new season. That situation only provided the push. I had made up my mind not to follow a man but to be led by the Spirit.

I do not share this story to expose my leaders. I share it show the face of spiritual abuse that runs a lot of our churches. This abuse happens when leaders are given authority in our life that is neither biblical nor healthy. The abuse robs you of your right to choose. It guilts you into decisions and shames you into following. The tool of manipulation disguises itself as spiritual counsel. We often accept this abuse in church culture because we are unaware it is not a system God set up.

I love my church. It is and will always be home, but I needed to step out and deal with me. It hurt to leave kids that trusted me to teach them. It hurt to not be apart of a flock I had help build. Stepping down from leadership meant I would be closed off by many I considered friends. It was not a choice I made out of anger rather I choice I took towards love.

The year I stepped down I was in the midst of planning my first trip to Africa. We began fundraising for the trip to Uganda that very month. I had signed up to go on the trip almost nonchalantly a few weeks before. The thought of money was not even a concern. My trip to Brazil was taken care of by a financial miracle. I have never met the person who paid for my trip to this day. The money came in last minute on the last day money was due.

I was happy to go to Africa. We had one fundraiser at a popular store called Sam's Club. It was cold outside and we were selling baked goods while asking for donations. We sang and entertained strangers all day. I saw a man I recognized so I asked if he would like to give to our cause. I was smiling, expecting him to have a hearty reaction. He half-smiled at the ladies avoiding eye contact with me.

The man gave a few dollars to our fund and walked away. The encounter saddened me. The ladies with me asked if I knew the man. It was obvious that what happened affected me. I told them yes. The man was a leader at my church. I had become a stranger only a week after resigning.

Lauryn Hill became my pastor for a season. Her album "MTV Unplugged" was my church. She has a song on this album called "I Get Out" that became my religion. I listened to that song from the time I woke up till I went to bed. It was in the car on my way to work and everywhere I went. The song was about getting free from bondage. The album is packed with songs of freedom. It made me hungry for that freedom. I would spend hours listening to the album and crying. I was caged. I had no idea how to get free, but I wanted it.

It was then that I picked up my pen again. I had not written in months. During this season, poetry poured out of me. I was writing about me. It had again become my release. I was writing to get free. Lauryn said on her album "if you give yourself up, nobody can blackmail you with anything." I wanted that type of freedom. I was writing to give myself up. I wanted the freedom to get free.

I visited a church one Sunday morning. As I sat in the magnificent building the thought rang in me, "The kings have built for there King a kingdom and their pastors reign in his place."

That day was sacrifice Sunday. I saw my sisters and cousins prepare their offerings for sacrifice. They were sacrificing for the building fund…the church full of people, mostly from the housing projects, sacrificing for a building…a building they could not eat in without permission…a building that would not house the poor. The funds would not feed the hungry. I was enraged at what I witnessed.

I saw people running to the altar, and it broke my heart. They attached their faith to money instead of His love. I thought about the indulgences of Martin Luther's day. I thought of the Mercedes the pastor drove that sat in front of the building. I was nearly sick and left immediately.

I began going to Akil's church for Sunday worship. They understood grace. I needed grace in this season. I was so happy when the time came to go to Africa. On the flight to Uganda I looked through past journal entries. One entry had a little note at the end of it saying I wanted to go to Northern Uganda someday. I do not remember writing it. That entry gave me a sense of expectancy for what was ahead. When I got to Africa, the earth came alive. My journal entries were simple:

"Alive…the place is alive….not just the people. Africa lives, and it moves you. Heaven is so much closer to the earth. The sky seems to be only a jump away, so close that if you leaped high enough you would be among the clouds. The earth wraps itself around you. The sun is a part of you and not some distant element. The wind speaks and the rain restores your sight, Africa is alive!"

About the people I wrote; "They are a black so beautiful it draws you in. Hearts so open and loving that you are offended at how it provokes you to see how jacked up your heart is. They would stare with the most intense and frightening stares and with a wave you usher in a smile that lights the world. Jesus lives in their smiles. Men who aren't ego stricken but who rather love and openly display their affections one to another in the most innocent and godly way."

The trip was like water, and I was a thirsty man. When we landed one of our hosts, a guy named Robert, grabbed my hand and interlocked our fingers. Here I was with a guy in the middle of the airport holding hands. I wondered if he was hitting on me. I thought he was he was bold to do it in front of everyone. I did not know it then but men holding hands was normal there.

After that day every one of them would grab my hand, and we would walk hand in hand interlocking fingers through the streets and in the mall. Small little gestures like that were healing me. I did not know what it was like to have a man hold my hand and love me purely brother to brother. There was no hiding behind sports and high fives. Affection was pure, and I did not lose me to get it.

There was one guy named Herman who became my brother. He was blunt and full of joy. He would grab my hand everywhere we went. Walking through stores or in communities, he was always by my side.

If anything was out of line he would ask, "Are these people Born Again?"

This difference in being Born Again and saved stuck with me.

These people knew what community was…for real. I shared a bed with Robert. My iPod became the property of whomever held it at the time. I was not a person on my own…I was a part of them. The way they touched me and held my hand was challenging what was in me. The love they expressed in affection rivaled the walls and the numbness. Change was calling.

Mother Africa
Stepping into darkness
Led by the light she brings
Told of the horrors she's seen
Feeling the pain it brings
Invited to come in and receive the love she holds
She extends her hands and embraces me, welcome!
"Webale Ssebo¹"...And tears fill my eyes
Webale and I feel I haven't done enough
She's only eaten one meal all day
Cause while the sun is out her and her children learn and play
Hoping that the sun will shade their hunger throughout the day
As regal as they come, my history in every inch of her being
She has given birth to what my eyes hold, and I want to hold her

Africa, Oh Mama Africa...
Can I Hold you as you embrace me
Uganda, Oh Mama. Uganda
Can I live in you as you live in me...
Africa...oh Africa...oh Mama Africa

Beautiful, Beautiful I wonder if they'd fall as much as I did when I
met you
Will they see the beauty in you I see
I wonder if they'll dream about you and realize they can't live
without you
Will their hearts beat with the vibrations of your sound
And if you were water would they drink you down
Can they embrace you as their past
And feel like they know who they are now...at last
Will you help them feel again...
I wonder if pride will rise in them...
For you, are Beauty not to be compared
Africa
Mama Africa

---

1   Thanks Sir

Chapter Fifteen
Moses and Lion

Pretender

Praying those prayers that make the strongest men weep
Teaching The Word in a way that makes it come alive
Like, Esther's walking right in front of you
You can smell the scent of hot unleavened bread in the wilderness...
Makes you wonder what quail taste like
He is anointed is what everyone says
When he opens his mouth to sing everyone stands
Hands lifted. Going in
He leads them in a place of worship that some have never experienced
Yet, When he leaves them and they are all gone away
He comes home and he peels away who he has been all day
He shows himself who he is
Hooking up with anyone who will take him on the DL
Using his hand to release the pressure he has built up
Watching what will allow him to escape
He feels alone because the pressures of his past consumes him
And so he lives a life putting on a show
Being who they think he is
Living how they think he lives in front of them
And the pressures of that life is killing him
Because when he releases
Either alone or with someone guilt and obligation pursue him
He can't continue how he is
He can't go to what he knows won't produce life
One day in a moment he wakes up sees where he is
He's been a pretender
Pretending that he has it all together
He cries in himself to hell with anything else
Give me what's real because I want to live he cries.
I want to live

The Uganda trip was full of adventure, including the food we were served. All of my teammates at some point had illness from the meals. The food had no affect on me. However, with the mosquitoes I was not so lucky. I stopped taking malaria medicine a few days into the trip. I then displayed indications of the virus. I was weak, sick and in pain.

We still continued with our programs and ministry. I would teach and minister for hours trying not to show I was ill. After teaching I would nearly collapse, lying on the ground until we went to our compound. After a few days I was treated in a local clinic and given medication.

After my bout with sickness we took a trip to Northern Uganda. We visited a place called Gulu. Our team was hosted by a well-known pastor. The place had become well-known by the documentary "The Invisible Children." The country had experienced horrific things. Their children were being taken from them and made to become child soldiers. Some children were even made to kill their parents. The documentary exposed that terror.

On our visit to Gulu, we toured the Internally Displaced People (IDP) Camps. After the tour, we stayed in a hotel in Gulu. The experience was frightening...the fear was tangible. The hotel was in the city center. Our American team was made up of four girls and me, the only male. Our guides for the trip were the pastor, his son, his assistant and our driver. The rooms were divided and I was given a room to myself.

Alone in my room, the stories that we had heard began to replay in my head. The day was exhausting so I tried to get some sleep. While I slept, I had vivid dreams causing me to wake up in near panic attacks. The dreams became real...like they were happening to me in real life. At times I could not tell the dreams from reality. Kids seemed to visit me that night. They were fearfully trying to escape being abducted.

As I lay in bed, the kids lay beside me above my head and even at times across my chest. They also hid under the bed. We silently became company for each other. Their fear became mine. The only thing that separated us from the abductors was a door. Those vivid depictions that seemed like reality made it a restless night. The experience stuck with me the remainder of the trip.

On the plane back ride back to the States it hit me that I was leaving a place that made me feel alive. I was returning to a world that trapped me. I nearly jumped out of my seat. The thought rang in me "What the heck are you doing? Why did you get on the plane?" I came home from my first trip to Africa haunted by what I had experienced. I shared my experiences with anyone that would listen.

For weeks the kids from Gulu seemed to haunt me. In the middle of the night they would surround me as I slept. This time there was no fear...they only served as a reminder. I could not forget them. I could not shake what I had experienced in the slums of Kampala or the joy that I had encountered in the churches. I was determined to get back.

That first trip was in the Spring, so I planned my second for the Fall. I was still working for the same organization that started the kids' ministry at my home church. While planning my trip my secret life was discovered by the organization's leader. It was a discovery that brought some freedom. However, it also brought contention.

Although I had already begun sharing my addiction and wounds from childhood with people, my employer still had no idea. That school year our theme message was "Treasures." The program dealt with taking off masks and looking into the mirror. In the program I would pull out a twenty dollar bill and ask the kids if they wanted it. Then I would ball it up, stomp on it and ask it they still wanted it. The question was always met with shouts of "Yes!" Then I would ask why they wanted it. The answer would always echo "It's still worth something!"

The programming again played a part in my life as it did while living with the family in previous years. I was already on the road to freedom and things covered were being exposed. There was no shame in the beginning…only relief. I had begun performing and doing poetry in clubs and cafes by then.

Most people already knew my struggle, but I think that discovery made it real to them. My poetry was not just words but real life issues being poured out. I was not only pouring it out to help others but to free myself from bondage.

The program and the season of life pushed me to keep exposing my lie. I was so ready to be free from the longings that still taunted me. I was the Program Coordinator for the organization by then. I had worked my way up in the organization. It had become a part of me, and I was intertwined with it.

I partnered with the organization for my next trip to Uganda. I traveled around sharing my stories of Uganda and gathered supplies and clothing to take back with me. My team this trip was more diverse. My good friends and co-workers traveled with me. This trip proved to be just as amazing as the last. I was challenged a lot while there. We met kids from Gulu, some were former child soldiers. Those kids were like wind refreshing me. They told me stories from their past. They shared stories of murdering their families and seeing death. When they finished with the horror they praised God that they were there.

These kids' stories seemed so unreal. There were two kids in particular that stuck out to me the first trip, Justin and Ocaya. These young men were brilliant and had such sweet spirits. After all the kids shared their stories with me I was to give them a message. I was honest with them and told them I did not know what to say. Justin chimed in and encouraged me. He told me to encourage them.

Justin shared that his mother was dying in the IDP camps of HIV while he was there at school. He said he wished he could take care of her but she wanted him there.

He then said, "Encourage me."
I shared with Justin a bit of my story of losing my mother. I told him about dropping out of school and then going back to get my G.E.D. and how my faith helped me through it all.

He then said, "Thank you. That helps me so much." It was hard to believe something so simple had any impact that Spring.

When we returned that Fall I was excited to see the kids from Gulu again. We arrived at the school and I spent time with the kids I was with earlier that year. Last time I was there Justin was just another one of the kids, but this time he was the leader. He was giving direction to the other kids. I was elated to see them all.

I talked with them about my poetry and shared that I had written about them. I told them how much they impacted my life. Then they began to share about how much our visit impacted them. Justin talked about the difference our conversation made in him. I was baffled at what he shared. I thought my words were just a shot in the dark, but to him they hit home.

The social worker that oversaw the kids was in tears as she talked about the difference in their behavior. I cried as she told me that they are so full of life now.
She exclaimed, "Justin dances." I sang the song that I wrote about Justin as my team members played instruments.

This trip to Uganda was just as amazing as the previous one. I was different in Africa. When home I was picky about food, but in Uganda I ate whatever they sat before us. While on the trip I talked to my co-workers about how my thoughts of work and life at home were shifting. I was sure I did not want to go back to life as normal but did not know what that meant for me. The trip ended and we went back home but my heart never left Africa.

The week I got home from Uganda I wrestled with what was next for me. I felt a shift in my season of work and life. I wrestled with quitting my job and doing something else, but I had no idea what that would be. I had been a speaker and performer for so long I did not know anything I was good at.

The weekend passed, and I was supposed to start work. I emailed asking what I needed for work. I was sent an email summoning me to a meeting. I knew that things were about to change for me, and I welcomed it. The meeting was at the organization leader's home.

When I arrived at the meeting I was met by her and the organization's Executive Director. We sat at her dining room table. At the end of the meeting, I was released from my contract. The release was based on fear that the reputation of the organization could be hindered if anyone found out about my issues.

The release brought a sense of peace. The same peace that washed over me when I resigned from the church now covered me. I left the meeting excited about what was ahead. I felt that a healthy change was coming. What I was discovering was that freedom was possible but not as neat as I expected.

I had worked for the organization all of my adult life. There was sadness of leaving the shows behind, but I was looking forward to what was ahead. There were so many possibilities. I had Africa in my heart, and poetry on my mind. I wanted to write and travel. I wanted to discover true freedom. I found the more I exposed my mess, the lighter the weight became.

A part of the freedom I desired was the ability to choose. For years, sex was not a choice for me…I needed it. I lacked the freedom to say no. The need was kin to a junky needing a hit from the pipe. I woke up with desire like an alcoholic needing a taste.

The longing stayed with me. Sometimes it was quieter than others, yet it was always in control.

I began to consider what was next for me. I did not know if I should just get a job or somehow get to Africa. I felt like I needed to hear from God. I felt God say that he would feed me from ravens. These ravens would be unexpected ways of provision. He began doing just that. The ravens were people from all over...some I had never met.

No one knew I no longer had a job. People began slipping money into my pocket. There were times when strangers would walk up to me and tell me, "God told me to give you this" and hand me a wad of cash. I also had friends who would hang out, leave, and then return with money telling me, "I don't know why, but God told me to turn around and give this..."

It seemed like everywhere I went someone would have a word of encouragement for me in this season of life. The words all would echo the same messages. Whether I was in church or hanging out somewhere the words kept coming. I began to expect them. In the church prophetic words or words of knowledge were common. For me the words were coming in unlikely places.

People would walk up to me and tell me I was either Moses or a Lion. Others would say I was meant to usher in liberation or justice. I could be in the back of a church meeting and someone would make their way to me and tell me what they felt the Lord said about me. Often saying you are a lion that will roar with Justice.

Once in a house church, a lady sang over me

"Here he comes, here he comes, he looks like a lion."

She sang of me traveling to the nations with a message of freedom and justice. I was getting the same words over and over from people I had never met in places I did not expect and all at different times.

The messages were not just in church or meetings.

I was at a movie theater one night and noticed a lady looking at me. Initially, I was freaked out by her staring. After catching her looking at me a few times I knew she had something to say. She finally walked over to my group and asked to talk to me.

She said, "I do not know if you believe in God speaking but he told me to tell you, you have a Spirit like Moses and you are going to lead people to freedom."
Amidst my bondage, I was being told I would be used to set people free. God's kingdom is upside down.

Once I traveled to Washington on a visit with a friend. While there we went to JHOP (Justice House of Prayer). We sat on the floor during worship. The leader was a young white guy in his early twenties. There were only a few of us in the room as he strummed his guitar singing.

Then the young man began to sing, "Moses take up your staff, Moses take up your staff."

I knew he was talking to me as soon as he said it. He opened his eyes and looked at me.

As our eyes met he said, "The Lord told me this song was for you." He again recited the refrain…I chuckled.

The words came so frequently. I would look at my friends, and they knew what was said. The words all came from strangers. Some would sing it…some would just speak it, but it was always "You are lion for Justice or Moses leading people to freedom". The words pushed me.
The more the words came, the more I wanted them to be true. I did not know if they were just for that season or my future, but I knew they meant something. In this season, poetry and music flowed. I

wroteand shared. I was eager to divvy up my mess if anyone would listen. I believed that freedom was possible.

I was pouring my story out. I was doing whatever I could to tell on myself. I did not care what people thought. I was not concerned if they would judge me. My life was my poetry, and my poetry was my life. When I spoke I was showing people me…flaws and all. I believed exposing my issues was my first step toward freedom.

My dad heard from my grandmother about what happened to me as a child. She learned it the day she heard me speak at church. I was a man in my twenties when he found out. I came to see him on one of his Nashville visits. He was staying at my uncle's house.

I could tell that something was on his mind. He seemed distracted the entire time I was there. He was not the playful guy he was normally around his brothers. My friend Micah and I visited for a while before deciding to take off. As we were leaving, he walked out behind us. He asked me to speak privately while Micah went to the car.

We stood in the front yard away from the house and car to talk. At first he seemed nervous then frustrated. He struggled to put together his words.

Finally he asked, "Did someone touch you when you were little?"

Calmly and somehow not even shocked by the comment, I told him yes.

My dad was overwhelmed with emotion. His eyes filled with tears. His anger and hurt were almost apparent. "Why didn't you tell me?" He asked. "Who was it? Tell me who it was, I will kill him," he exclaimed, not giving me time to answer the first question. It had been many years since the incident in the Jacuzzi.

"It was a long time ago," I told him. "I moved on and you should too."

He tried to get more answers out of me.

I calmly told him, "Dad it's over…it's the past, and I am not talking about this with you."

Although I pretended the conversation was casual it meant a lot. For the first time in years I felt my father's love for me. In his concern and anger, I could see he cared. We never spoke of it again.

Known

He heard the word…
"I know that it feels hard and it's so tough now, but if you would
hold on change is coming"
And it moved him to tears
It brought a glimpse of light to what seemed deem
Someone knows, he thinks…
Cause he feels alone…
Carrying what most never understand
Words that part his lips born through pain
A view of life he cannot at time convey
It is far bigger than you, he hears God say
But he feels at times he carries it alone
Sometimes those that walk with him just don't understand
I see God in you they say, yet so quick they run away
"I know that it feels hard…" a feeling he tries to hide
It's harder than you think, the call he walks alone
Because sometimes it's only God that can understand
Friends don't realize that sometimes they are all he has
And their turns, and words cut deeper than they know
And he bares the reproach…
Of the dislike of strangers who can't understand the justice in his
poetry
They'd rather have service and go home feeling good
Crying silently, I only told them what I hear You say
The reproach…
Of leaving a nation he has always known
Aren't there people you can help, here!
He heard the word…
"I know that it feels hard and it's so tough now, but if you would
hold on change is coming"
And it waits for direction…
Realizing that the One who speaks thinks higher than man
And that sometimes it's only Him that can hold his hand…
He thinks…You know me!

Chapter 16
Gotta Get Free

Write Poet

Write Poet. Friend Poet. Brother Poet.
Hold not back words...
Write until your poetry resurrects the dead
And causes those alive to live
Write until dreams become memories, lived.
Passions becomes occupation and sacrifice meets celebration.
Write until you sit with gods...
Until like Homer you are mentioned with the greats and held in honor
Until your words become flesh and redeem lost.
Write until the dead rise and the dumb speak
Write until we know we're free
Until we see, until words become swords and slay giants that oppress
Until you deplete your pen and then scream.
Words Be Light. Be Life.
Scream until dry bones live
Words. Poetry
Until men rise from tombs, and women from graves
Until kids are no longer slaves
Scream until you are free
Until they hear Me
Until they yell, He Spoke that Word, Spoken Word
Poet And they see
The Poet was always Me.

The release from my job and resignation from church were like letters of emancipation. For the first time since I was a kid I was independent. I was allowed to do whatever I wanted. I was completely liberated to make choices on my own that would only reflect on me. I felt like I was free to get free.

I wanted to see what life was really meant to be. I realized I was living in a false reality. For me, my church's mode of operation held no life. I wanted to live free without any covers…to be exactly who I was, whoever I was. I accepted the opportunity to divulge and live my truth.

During this season I adopted the saying, "To hell with anything else, give me what's real." I wanted to live.

I was seeking a new reality. I wanted freedom from my religious ways of thinking…a lifestyle rooted in obligation and tradition. I wanted release from the longings that held me.

There were teachings that I heard in that time that stirred me. One was about God drawing lines. The gentleman spoke about the lines or boundaries that God drew and how they were different for each person. He spoke about there being absolute sins but also some areas where things are gray and not so black and white.

The message provoked me. I started to look at my life and what I participated in and refrained from. I realized I was living within lines someone had drawn. Lines etched out in their fears and ignorance. I was surviving based on how a system of tradition viewed God rather than His history and my encounters.

Another teaching came from a good friend and mentor. He has one of the most amazing ways of looking at the Garden of Eden. I am not great on expounding on his teaching, but I will share what I gleaned. He talked about the trees that were in the garden: the Tree of Life and the Tree of the Knowledge of Good and Evil (TKGE) .

He centers in on the fact that Adam and Eve were free to eat from any tree in the garden except TKGE.

The trees serve as a backdrop to a hidden truth as he teaches. God laid the opportunity to choose before Adam and Eve. While giving them the freedom to choose He also instructs them not to partake of one tree, TKGE. The Tree of the Knowledge of Good and Evil represented the responsibility to judge or discern what is right (good) and what was wrong (evil). It was a responsibility they were not meant to take on.

The teaching was also about perspective...the story of Joseph painting his picture. In Joseph's life most would have deemed his being sold into slavery, his time in Potiphar's house or imprisoned as bad. Yet what Joseph echoed in the end was what was seen as bad God used as good. We do not have God's vantage point nor His perspective...a fact that leaves us ill-equipped to discern in and of ourselves the good from evil.

Sitting and listening to these teachings I realized I had been eating from the wrong tree. I had built my life around the Tree of the Knowledge of Good and Evil. It all then became so simple. Jesus had come to give me life. Instead of following life, I had chosen religion.

Religion is a man made system set up to govern a predetermined standard of living...a standard that came from truths but held little to no room or understanding of grace. I had chosen to live within these walls of determining for myself and others what was (right) good and what was (wrong) evil. I had to learn that was not my job. It was God's job to judge good and evil.

I needed God to draw new lines. I wanted Him to take the responsibility to decipher good from evil. I needed to allow God to partner the Truth of the scripture with His grace. It had been rehearsed throughout the Scripture that we should be led by the Spirit, but I found myself being led by human thoughts and perception. I took on a new way of thinking. I would ask myself questions like; "Did God draw this line? Did God say I couldn't do this? Did God say I could not go here?"

It seems so elementary now, but I needed to unplug from the system I had grown so accustomed to living in. I had to learn with each person there are different lines. Each one of us has different encounters, and what is good for one person could be detrimental to the other. Yes, there are absolutes, but not everything is as black and white as I had believed.

Take alcohol for instance. Drinking had been demonized for me in ministry. Religion had drawn the line of alcohol being evil. That was not God. I was free to have a glass of wine without guilt or shame. (I realize though that was not a line for me. There are people who should not drink…those for whom alcohol is a problem. I also realize that in some cultures the demonizing and/or abuse of alcohol has an impact on whether one chooses to drink or not. See, it's not so black and white.)

I was finding that when God drew lines His lines were life giving. His restrictions were because He loved us and did not want us hurt. I needed to know for me what those lines were. I challenged what I had been taught over the years. I went to the Bible and wanted truth.

I found a simple truth…God calls us to be led by the Spirit. Being Spirit-led was evidence of relationship. All these religious rules and boundaries I lived under opposed the freedom He came to give. I found that many leaders have a God-complex. We don't trust that the Holy Spirit is able to lead and correct, so we set up lines and boundaries to do his job.

To hell with anything else, I wanted to know truth for myself. This was the journey of digging into the lies to find the truth. I began to dig into the lies I believed about church and about myself. The religious way of living destroyed my life. The mask was being confronted with truth.

For me, freedom was not coming with a slap of oil on my forehead. It did not happen with a healing prayer, but it was becoming a journey…an exploit full of mistakes and tears. Along the way I have met so many people that wipe the haze from my eyes.

I found myself in places that I would have never been in years before, and I waited for God to draw the lines. I was like a teenager who finally had tasted freedom. I wanted to take advantage of it. I was on a mission.

A couple of my church friends and I went to a local club. It was a place that I would have never wanted to be caught dead in, in prior years. In this place I saw people from diverse backgrounds, different ethnicities, and sexual preferences. Some dressed up; others wore barely anything. There were even those who you wondered if they were male or female. However, they were all completely fine with being who they were.

Though it conflicted with a lot of what I had been taught over the years the thought rang in me, "What if the church was a place where people could come and feel free to expose who they are? What if it was a place that provoked vulnerability instead of conformity?"

I am sure the church would not look like the club we were in, but it would challenge us to seek God and not the approval of men.

I was experimenting with things I would have never done. I even tried weed for the first time. I had no idea who I was yet, but I desired to know. I needed to know who I was inside all the lies I had lived. I was talking to people I would never given time to in previous years…those I had before demonized because of their lifestyle or views.

One day after a night at the club an old friend from high school called me up. He asked me plainly, "What are you doing?" In reference to hanging out at the club. In that moment I was dumbfounded. I told him honestly I did not know.

What I did know was I spent all those years in church and did not know who I was. I knew I did not fit into the clubbing lifestyle. It became obvious after a while. I had to drink a lot just to be able to get comfortable. After a while I felt a line being drawn in me. It was not who I was. God was speaking to me about who I was and was not.

There were absolute boundaries that I did not push, but lines that were not clear I tested. This methodology I would not recommend. In my pursuit of discovery I made a lot of bad choices. I was not always wise. I did not always wait for God's leading.

I was meeting people who were on their own journeys. I was like a magnet for people who wanted to get free. I still struggled some, but I was learning.

I met people who struggled their whole lives with homosexuality and wanted to be free. It was a concept I did not understand. I had no idea who I was. I wondered how someone who knew who they were could reject it. I realized that their journey was not mine. I did not have answers but I knew The Answer. I was encountering a God whose love surpassed sexual preference.

I was discovering people that knew Jesus while struggling with who they were. Their struggles were not because of an issue with Him, but they had somewhere down the line believed a lie…lies streaming from pulpits and conferences…lies that were instilled through abuse or spoken over them as children. Not all struggles were sexual, some were emotional or mental.

What I knew for a fact was that the Holy Spirit was alive and still able to speak. The church as it was did not provide a place for brokenness that lead to healing. I found so many wounded men along the way... those whose wounds spilled into everything they did.

The conversation of what happens to a boy that is molested never happens in church. If you have sex with a man you are thought to struggle with homosexuality. If that is deemed the case then we create a ministry to undo that. In the church we create programs to deal with symptoms. However, we have little clue how to deal with the root of the issue.

The men I encountered along the way were like me...we wounded men were once broken boys...suffering silently in our guilt...like so many people who sit in churches, hurting yet unable to speak. These men build walls against Jesus because of anger at the church...men who struggle to see they are worth loving...struggle to see they have value outside of the sexual gratification they give others.

I spent all those years in church yet did not know how to love me so I was giving me away. I needed to know I was worth something. I realized I had been sick for so long that I did not know how to be well. I still gave in to longings, sometimes out of routine.

Seeing so many wounded around me was overwhelming. I was frustrated with who I was. I hated not being totally over my issues. I wanted to hit a restart button on life. I felt I needed to escape...I needed a way out. I had been caged so long I did not know how to fly without hurting myself or others.

Africa was still on my mind. I would daydream about the kids often. My friends would joke when I did not respond to a question immediately that I was gone to Africa. They were often right. My mind was in the huts of Uganda. I was dreaming of dancing with the kids in dirt floor churches. I missed the people and culture.

I needed Africa far more than it needed me. So I set out back to Africa. When I got there, I realized quickly I could not run from myself. The demons I carried were not territorial but demons that had accompanied me from childhood. They entered at my breaking point. My demons were a part of me.

I needed to confront me. I could not run or start over. I realized that as I ran from bondage and the chore of facing myself I was avoiding God. I was so scared that if I gave my heart to God fully again I would be tied up again in religion. I was scared to look at the mess I had made with my mistakes. I stopped worrying about the lines and the trees and just wanted to exist.

Running from church left a lot of time to consider things. I thought about my mother dying from HIV. The letters had always provoked fear in me. I had made up my mind to be tested. I had been tested before, but the test always brought back painful memories. When I took the test I had settled in my heart I would kill myself if I had the virus. I know God is forgiving, but our bodies are not always. I did not want to suffer like she had. I was elated to find out I was negative.

The fact that suicide entered into my mind began to get to me. I was running from religion by avoiding God. I wanted who I was, but I feared the lines would be too many. I was scared of returning to my old ways. I was scared he would lead me back to chains.

Music again showed her face in my life. I was watching a show mentioning India Arie's album. For some reason I knew I had to download it. It blew me away. Jesus spoke to me so clearly through the music.

There was one song in particular that hit home for me. The title is "River Rise." The lyrics, "River Rise, Carry me back home, I cannot remember the way. River rise and carry me back home, I surrender today." Those words struck in me like chords. I remembered the time with God when he broke the sadness in my heart after my mother died. I remembered the freedom from grief He brought.

I listened to that song like it was a prayer. I wanted the River of Life to rise in me again. I started sharing with God my fears of Him and religion. Honesty is good, especially with God. One thing I know for sure, He cares enough to meet you where you are. But you have to be willing to not stay where you are. I was renewed and ready to continue my journey.

My Reality (Excerpt)

Twelve years old was a long time ago...So it seems
But to me it was just yesterday
My today is baked in the oven of a past I hide with a smile and a
Poem
I have moved on... it didn't kill me...yet I am learning to become
stronger
Cause the strength I adopted as a child made me weak...On the
inside
I was just a child and be strong they said
But no one was strong for me
My Reality...
Waking up in the middle of the night to gun fights
HIV just as common as a cold
Christmas stolen by an uncle who wants to get high
Sex was just as common for a 5 year old as for his parents
No one protects your innocence
I was called a man before I ever saw what one looked like for real
And fathers...they only exist in fairy tales
Cause they are never really around
So you imagine what it would be like if Daddy stayed!
This is the reality that I was born and reared in
And so I try like Will Thatcher to change my stars
Believing against what I see
There is something better for me too
Because on one end I struggle with who I am
My father never told me
His father never told him
So I struggled secretly
Secret struggles that led to secret sins
But I am Tired of hiding the fact that I too hurt and yes I too have
issues
I am learning to give myself up
Pressing for change...

Chapter 17
Wounded Healer

My Reality (Excerpt)

He is like a potter and he sits us on his wheel
And he makes us again another...
Where there is a mar he adds water and he smooths it out
Where there has been hurt he presses down until the scars can no
longer be seen by the eye
With care and concern he fashions us to be what we are meant to
be
He knows that some vessels take longer than others
But with patience and the care of a father he molds us...
I know your jacked up but just sit a while...He has you
I know it hurts but stay on the wheel He is molding you
You will not look the same
And as we spin in this life he adds and he takes away
What will come out will be different
I may look like a hunk of clay now but don't touch me...I'm still in
the process
When he finishes there will be a new reality!
When he finishes we will be who we are meant to be
When it's done there will be a change inside!

Telling my lie was my first step, but it only provided a table of opportunity. In order for me to partake of the freedom I desired I needed to deal with what I set on that table. What I learned was God likes to sit at the table with us. He gladly plunges into our mess with us.

He chooses to dive into what we have created so He can redeem. There is no mess that God cannot turn into a message. We have not been in something so long that He cannot set us free from it. I was sharing my symptoms, but He wanted to address the unseen. He wanted to deal with the hidden stuff in me. I was carrying stuff in my heart that years of avoidance was covering.

There were a lot of unseen things. I began to pray God would help me deal with my mess. He began to meet me. I had so much in me that I did not know existed…so many lies and hurts that I still harbored. I had been strong for too long, and I needed to be broken enough to heal. God was at work in my heart and character.

I was bombarded with fear-filled thoughts. I started having intense thoughts of death. I was surprised I was still alive. I realized I was living my life waiting to die and did not know it. I expected to die by the age my mother was when she died. Subconsciously, I awaited that death. I began having dreams and visions of myself in a casket. Thoughts of death haunted me.

I started having visual pictures of the faces of people I had slept with. Along with the visions came this overwhelming sense of shame and guilt. I started to remember things I had forgotten over the years. The visions came more as accusations than memories.

I remember vivid pictures of myself in sexual situations…pictures going all the way back to my childhood. Some visions were accompanied by fear. I would wake up in the night and feel this sense of darkness around me. There were nights when I was aware of a presence in the room other than myself. I would look around the room and just know someone else was there. I thought I was losing my mind. This shame and guilt was heavy.

The dreams intensified and with it also the fear. I would cry and beg God for mercy. I spent hours praying, asking God to forgive me. After I asked for forgiveness for one thing, another memory would come. This continued for some time.

I talked to my good friend and mentor about it. He told me to step into it...face it. I was to face death with the knowledge that if I die I go to Jesus. He told me not to give into it but face that fear with faith. I took his advice.

I was in the midst of the Fire of God. It felt like God had turned the heat up. It was a season of purging. God was challenging me to confront me. The fire caused me to deal with the mess I made behind my mask. I also had to take responsibility for my actions. I had to own my choices as my own. I had to share in the blame before I gave it to Him to forgive.

I continued to ask forgiveness of all the memories that bombarded me. As I faced it with assurance of forgiveness the fear left. God was using that time to free me of the guilt and shame I held. I had never really looked into my past because I was ashamed of myself. My past was being brought right to me. When it came so did God's love to forgive me along with the grace to forgive myself.

All those years I was using sex to fill voids in me…voids of love and acceptance. When a child is taken advantage of that child is robbed of their innocence. Mine was stripped in childhood. I served my sex longing without regard to myself but also without account of others. I was ashamed of myself. In my years of servitude I had careless sex with so many others without regard for their feelings. I hated myself.

I had not cared about the heart of others or what wounds they carried.

That feeling grieved me. The shame of that was being dealt with. God was showing it to me so I could confess and let it go. I had to forgive myself. I had to let go of the guilt of my encounters. The fear in the beginning had me thinking it was the Devil himself. But God can use what feels like the enemy's accusations of guilt to reveal truth. If there was fear I stepped into it and challenged it with His love. His love was always stronger.

I had to let go of my past to reach for what was ahead. I had to let go of the weight. The shame and guilt had followed me for years, whispering. It whispered my disgrace. Telling me I did not deserve a better life. In all actuality I probably did not deserve a better life. Thank God that He does not deal with me based on what I deserve.

So often we live subject to guilt and shame and cannot move forward because of it. Facing it and dealing with it allowed me to let it go. Being broken for so long sometimes you struggle to live healed. I made mistakes that would teach me a lot. Someone once said, "Hurt People, Hurt people." I knew that to be truth in my life.

I was living all those years in hurt. I hurt many people along the way. Not only within friendship but also in my secret life. I was using my body as an investment, hoping to gain from each encounter...hoping that somehow what I was giving would be enough for someone to choose me.

I wondered where the desire to be chosen by someone came from. As I prayed and really dove into my mess I started to hit the roots of some of my issues. Over time I would have revealing memories. One was of my dad leaving. I was outside the vehicle that was to take my dad to Indiana. It was the day after my mother's funeral. My dad was about to pull off to head back home.

With the memory came perspective. I felt like my dad did not choose me in that moment. I had believed the lie that I was not worth choosing. It was not a conscious belief but one I lived out in my actions. When my dad went back home he would be met by "his new family." I was replaced by his wife and my younger brother. I believed he had chosen them over me.

I began to revisit my past. I considered past events to gain a different perspective. I was learning that God could speak through the wounds of my past to bring healing. This serves as a new way to bring mess to the table for God to redeem.

I thought about how I felt when I was touched as a child…looked at the longing to be touched. Contemplated why I would risk my life, having sex just to feel like someone wanted me. I thought about Woody so many years before and how my heart had been broken in that situation…the feelings of not being wanted or loved back…the co-dependency I displayed. These together were wounds that begin to stain the man I had become. They took part in me becoming the wounded man I was.

I had to let go of those hurts and accept new truths. I had to believe that I had worth and was worth choosing. I had to learn to love myself. All these years I thought I loved me…but I had not. I realized the only thing I thought I brought to the table in the past was a penis and a personality. I had to teach myself that I was more than that. I needed to choose to believe that I had worth. The journey to me had begun.

This has become a daily choosing. Getting free for me is a choice. I have to choose Life over death daily. I have to choose me over gratifying someone else…choose God to lead me as opposed to going at it on my own. It is not always easy but has to be my way of life.

I weigh my decisions on what I am trying to get out of it. I seek to have the right motivation. I decide on whether or not the end result of even the smallest choice would yield life. I question if I would still celebrate me after I made a choice.

I am still on my journey to get free…still discovering new lies to conquer with Truth. I have learned to allow myself and others grace to heal. With every step I take walking in light, I whisper to my darkness "I am stronger now".

Freedom and healing is coming for me within community. It is coming in the counsel of those that I trust to speak into my life. Freedom does not mean I do not fall, but it gives me the right not too. Freedom gives me the authority to live a whole and healthy life. I realize the importance of asking for help with my inner turmoil.

What I have found over the years is that the more I share my story, the stronger I become. I am finding more and more that His kindness leads us to repentance. It's His grace that keeps me getting up and running back to Him. The Broken Boy is gone…the Wounded Man that was..is now a Wounded Healer…sharing my wounds hoping that it will help someone else.

I am often asked "How do you get free?"…people of all walks in life male and female. Their issues are not always sexual addiction or religion but they are entrapped to some sort of bondage. Often in Christendom we take what worked for us and make it into a formula. I have yet to see a formula work for everyone.

For me freedom has become a choice. My lines may differ from yours. The journey I am on is specific to me. The journey you walk is your own. I have chosen to walk in a way that yields life. It is not coming through brainwashing or fear of certain places. My choices are no longer syphoned through tradition or religion.

The key to freedom for me has been a journey full of grace. The journey that I am on of healing and letting go has only been possible because I trust God to lead me. I give myself the grace to fall. I remind myself that the truth is I do not have to. I surrounded myself with those who call me up into who I am instead of calling me out on my flaws. Freedom: allows me not to be perfect; grants me the grace to be flawed yet willing to be led. Freedom is possible...but sometimes it's messy. You need people to walk through it with you. I need Jesus.

I say Wounded Healer because I share where I was wounded in hopes someone will see healing is possible. I refuse to cover wounds and pretend they do not exist. I don't want to pretend it is not possible for me to fall or make mistakes. I wore too many masks for too long. I am a Wounded Healer because I have seen how wounds can heal. I have seen even in Jesus how His wounds brought redemption and healing to all humanity. We would not have Him cover the scars He bore for us. Then why do we cover ours?

So many people suffer secretly with their struggles. So many men are overlooked when it comes to sex abuse because they are male. If a female teacher has sex with a male student it is not taken that seriously. We in so many ways call our sons into manhood before their time. We look over these encounters and high-five the behavior. We have to deem our son's innocence worthy of protecting.

Conversations need to be had in our communities about the wounds that our young men bear. I struggled silently for years, and I was not alone. Countless young men suffer silently and secretly with their demons. Often showing up in hyper-sexuality, addictions and withdrawal. We often deem it as just who men are...but I beg to differ.

There are broken boys that we see day in and out. We teach them and train them on our football teams. They serve us at restaurants and live in our homes. These broken boys become wounded men. If these broken boys do not have a place to come and talk, their wounds carry over.

These wounded men become husbands and teachers. They are boyfriends to our daughters and our closest friends. If they continue in silence it will spill into everything they do. They become abusive to themselves and others. Wounded men wear masks because they do not know what real love is. They cover their hurts with masks of masculinity and even abuse of others. They mask hurt with ministry, success and perfectionism.

We can sit silently as our sons are molested in churches, schools or even sport camps. We can watch as they suffer silently...or we can talk. Healing and Freedom are possible, but we have to open the conversations. There has to be a place where wounded people come and let down their guards...a place where we stop pretending and wearing mask...a place in our homes, schools and places of worship.

This issue is not solely a church issue. Countless young men need freedom. The world is full of young men who need a place to share their brokenness...a place not to be judged for their mistakes and short- comings but to be called into their potential. I am not speaking of a building...I am speaking of an opportunity.

There has to be a space for conversation and the willingness to walk out life with our sons and brothers. What I found on my journey is the more I get free the freer people become around. The more I expose what I covered behind my mask the more others share that same freedom. I am learning that Free people, Free people.

I am still on my journey...still sitting at the table with God. I have gained new perspectives. I am learning who I am. I am less of a mess, but God is still dealing with me everyday. I know now, Freedom is possible...but it is messy. Grace and Truth aid us. We have to choose life daily...sometimes hourly...choose to believe we are worthy to love and to be loved.

The Potter

He calls as I come
Heart crying, come!
Broken like cup
Vessel
Pouring into me
Filling cracks
He, shapes me
I sing
Heart songs
In moans
Sway and hands waving
Tears flow
He like potter
Takes heart
Molding with grace
Hands speaking love
Embrace
Presence overwhelming
I like clay
Yield
Eyes open
He is here
Nothing exist but Him
Loved
Acceptance
Calling me
Into how He sees me
This is worship

CPSIA information can be obtained
at www.ICGtesting.com
Printed in the USA
LVOW11s0331131117
556067LV00002B/103/P